Poetry ExplorerS 2009

Leicestershire & Nottinghamshire

Edited by Mark Richardson & Lisa Adlam

First published in Great Britain in 2010 by

 Young**Writers**

Remus House
Coltsfoot Drive
Peterborough
PE2 9JX
Telephone: 01733 890066
Website: www.youngwriters.co.uk

Foreword

At Young Writers our defining aim is to promote an enjoyment of reading and writing amongst children and young adults. By giving aspiring poets the opportunity to see their work in print, their love of the written word as well as confidence in their own abilities has the chance to blossom.

Our latest competition Poetry Explorers was designed to introduce primary school children to the wonders of creative expression. They were given free reign to write on any theme and in any style, thus encouraging them to use and explore a variety of different poetic forms.

We are proud to present the resulting collection of regional anthologies which are an excellent showcase of young writing talent. With such a diverse range of entries received, the selection process was difficult yet very rewarding. From comical rhymes to poignant verses, there is plenty to entertain and inspire within these pages. We hope you agree that this collection bursting with imagination is one to treasure.

Contents

St Mary's RC Primary School, Loughborough

Thringstone Primary School, Coalville

Thurlaston CE Primary School, Thurlaston

Welbeck Primary School, Nottingham

Wolvey CE Primary School, Hinckley

The Poems

It's Hard To Say Goodbye

I woke up in the countryside,
My mother sent me here to hide.
It's hard to say goodbye in the middle of a fight,
When all you're worrying about is if your mum will be alright.
I never thought this day would come,
When I'm left alone without my mum.
It's hard to say goodbye.

I'm very joyful to say,
At least I have a place to stay.
Now I have to leave my newly-made friends,
When I get home I hope this war ends.
It's hard to say all your goodbyes,
When at your destination there may be a surprise.
It's hard to say goodbye.

Maddie Storey (10) & Georgia Crooks (11)
Abbey Road Primary School, Nottingham

Wartime

Evacuation,
Perpetual bombs falling,
More men lie defunct,
Excessive ear-splitting guns,
Excruciating men combat!

Euan Wilson (10) & Connor Cruickshank (11)
Abbey Road Primary School, Nottingham

Christmas At War

Christmas isn't Christmas when a war is going on.
Father is out fighting and Grandma is gone.
Everyone is terrified, mothers, fathers, girls and boys.
How can it be Christmas without Santa and our toys?

Christmas isn't Christmas when a war is going on.
No Christmas dinner, no happiness, what is going wrong?
A room with no tree, a fire with no log,
Christmas isn't Christmas when a war is going on.

Christmas isn't Christmas when a war is going on.
I pray for the day when all this sadness is gone.
Mother says, 'Don't worry, I'm sure it won't be long.'
Christmas can be Christmas after the war is gone.

Shania Hashmi & Ellen Blanche Morgan (10)
Abbey Road Primary School, Nottingham

Why?

Why do some people not give a care,
when some people are starving and dying out there?

Why do some people wish for guns to fire,
when people get shot, get hurt and expire?

Why do some people just want more,
When some people are dying with blood and gore?

Why are some people so greedy
when others are living in poverty?

Does anyone think of how the other half live,
the thing I ask is, 'Why?'

Emily Luk (10)
Abbey Road Primary School, Nottingham

Evacuees

Today I'm going away,
They say it's a long holiday.
My mother has a tear in her eye,
But if it's a holiday, why should she cry?

Today I'm going away,
I don't really want to go,
But my mum she just said no!
She said, 'It's best for you,
They might send me away too.'
Today I'm going away.

Iqra Hyder & Emily Luk (10)
Abbey Road Primary School, Nottingham

Boom, Bang, Pow!

Boom, bang, pow, bombs crash,
Boom bang, pow, bombs everywhere.
Bombs are crashing down,
Killing people all around.
Boom, bang, bombs fall here and there.

Hear the *crash, bang, smash,*
Crash, bang, smash, bullets fire.
Bullets everywhere,
Killing people all around.
Crash, bang, smash, the soldiers die!

Tarun Mistry & Lucy Jepson (10)
Abbey Road Primary School, Nottingham

War - Haiku

England is at war,
Germany is fighting back,
What will happen next?

Madeline Storey (10)
Abbey Road Primary School, Nottingham

3

YoungWriters

Colours Of War

Red is for the blood that spilled on the ground,
You can hear the bombs exploding all around.

Blue is the sea, where the navy has come.
All those lives lost so far away.

Green is for the army that marched all that way,
To fight Hitler's soldiers every single day.

Silver is for the bombers' moon,
Which helped them get away,
With bombing all the houses and killing in every way.

Mojghan Omid (10)
Abbey Road Primary School, Nottingham

The Colours Of War

Red is for the blood, pouring to the floor,
From all the blood and gore.
White is for the soldiers who fought side by side,
But sadly they had nowhere to hide.
Blue is for the skies clearing up after all the terrible war.
After victory, hopefully, there'll be no more.
Orange is for food that we all need to share,
Otherwise all the soldiers will think it's unfair.
Silver is for all the weapons that the soldiers fought with,
To help them and everyone around them live.

Tavleen Virdi & Miles Cliff (11)
Abbey Road Primary School, Nottingham

Haiku

Planes fly, bombs crash down
People dying in the crowd
Flowers turning brown.

Lizzie Berridge & Amelia Wills (10)
Abbey Road Primary School, Nottingham

Bombs

The bombs are ebony,
The bombs are life,
The bombs are terrifying,
They killed my wife!

My house was exploded,
When I came back from war,
The bombs are now coming, more and more . . .

They killed my wife,
It should have been me!

Sophie Hashmi & Fenella Symes (10)
Abbey Road Primary School, Nottingham

The Colours Of War

Black is for the bullets that are falling from the air,
Everyone's heading for shelter, this war's not fair.

Red is the anger Germans have against us,
Everyone is scared, all in a fuss.

Brown is the colour of the soldiers' uniform,
All in a bed, squished up in a dorm.

White is for peace, the war has ended,
We can now settle down while everything's mended.

Georgia Crooks (11) & Gemma Hay (10)
Abbey Road Primary School, Nottingham

Battlefield

Bullets are fired.
The mud is stained faint scarlet,
Dyed by soldiers' blood.
The battlefield is silent.
This war is never-ending.

Ellen Morgan (10)
Abbey Road Primary School, Nottingham

The Colours Of War

Red is for the blood that was lost from our men.
The gunshots killed many, again and again.

Orange is for the fire that burnt our homes.
The soldiers hit the floor with the blood and the bones.

Blue is for the sky that turned to smoke.
The civilians in their beds began to choke.

Silver is for the bullets, from the gun to the chest.
Our soldiers were tired, they needed to rest.

Taha Ali & Robert Brierley (10)
Abbey Road Primary School, Nottingham

The Colours Of War

Red is the blood the courageous soldiers shed,
Who lived and died in battle
Against the army Hitler led.
Green is for the tanks, their work is never done.
They will help us fight until this war is won.
Silver is for the shelters that make sure we survive,
But the soldiers who are fighting, don't have anywhere to hide.
Brown is for the mud where the soldiers have to stay,
Trying their best to keep the Germans out at bay.

Ellen Morgan & Fenella Symes (10)
Abbey Road Primary School, Nottingham

Blitz

Searchlights are swerving
And the sirens are sounding.
People are screaming,
It's a threatening sound,
The explosions are everywhere.

Harry Guttridge (10)
Abbey Road Primary School, Nottingham

Bombs

The bombs are falling,
And the sirens are bawling.
Bombers are coming,
And the people are running.
Run with the others,
Yes, run away to cover.
The bombs are falling,
And the sirens are bawling,
In England, war is calling.

Matthew Barrs (10) & Joshua Hutson (11)
Abbey Road Primary School, Nottingham

War

Guns are firing,
Shells are destroying armies,
Soldiers are dying.

Ella Smith & Jack Harmer (10)
Abbey Road Primary School, Nottingham

Victory

Flag is being raised,
Victory, we've won the war!
The Germans are gone.

Fenella Symes & Emily Luk (10)
Abbey Road Primary School, Nottingham

On My Bike

I was riding my bike
and what could I see?
The cars and the bikes
yelling at me.

I was riding my bike
and what could I see?
All the trees
blowing in the breeze.

I was riding in the market
and what could I see?
The shopkeepers yelling,
'Do you want anything to eat?'

I was riding my bike
and what could I see?
All the bees
trying to sting me.

Diyen Dhanak (10)
Abington High School, Wigston

Happiness Poem

Happiness is the colour yellow
and light baby pink.
It's the sound of waves
on a bright, blue sky day.

Happiness is the flavour of banana ice cream
with chocolate on top.
It's a love heart,
filled with hearts and smiles.

Happiness is banana
with strawberry smoothies all around.
It smells like a rose-scented candle
with a strawberry twist.

Happiness is a rose pink smoothie
that tastes like strawberries.

Jessica Nowell (10)
Abington High School, Wigston

What I Love To See!

I like to see my mum always glad,
I hate to see it when everyone's sad,

I like to see the world always sunny,
I like to see everybody with money,

I like to see all the birds in the trees,
I like to see lots of buzzy bees,

I love to see snow on the ground,
All the children running around,

I like to see all the fish in the ocean,
Swimming majestically without fuss or commotion,

But the best thing has to be,
The fact that I can see!

Matthew Zara (10)
Abington High School, Wigston

Fear Is . . .

A no hope grey
It's a taste of really nothing
Fear is like you're a tiny mouse
Crying out
But nobody can hear you
It's someone pulling down
On a blackboard
Fear,
It's the disastrous smell of death
It's the searing pain
Knowing you're thrown off board
Fear is . . .
Something you can't control
Because it's
Fear . . . !

Caitlin Goodall (10)
Abington High School, Wigston

Scary Things

Fear smells like a million worries running into your mind,
Fear sounds like a heartbeat getting louder and louder,
Fear looks like blood rushing into your eyes,
Fear tastes like red-hot lava,
Fear feels like all you want to do is give up,
Terror smells like there is someone after you,
Terror sounds like four knocks on the door and then you know
                                        there's trouble,
Terror looks like that monster under your bed,
Terror tastes like endless nothingness,
Terror feels like you've just missed a heartbeat.

Joseph Chamberlain (10)
Abington High School, Wigston

Bumbling Along

I can see . . .
A yellow and black buzzing bee
Flying through the blue sky.

I can see
My brother playing the guitar
Inconsolably in the melancholy atmosphere.

I can see
A scorching, yellow, hot sun
Blazing in the high sky
Among the fluffy sheep-like clouds.

Laurentta Echiejile (10)
Abington High School, Wigston

I Can Hear . . .

I can hear walking,
I can hear cars,
I can hear people all the way from the park.

I can hear bees,
I can hear rain going down the drain.

I can hear the wind,
I can hear cracking from a nut in a tree.

I can hear talking,
I can hear rustling from the trees.

Roshni Bhalla (10)
Abington High School, Wigston

I Wonder What Wonder

I wonder what wonder feels like?
I bet it feels rough and hard.
I wonder what wonder tastes like?
I bet it tastes bumpy and soft.
I wonder what wonder looks like?
I think it looks like mould.
I wonder what wonder sounds like?
I think it sounds like someone all buzzing with questions.
I wonder what wonder smells like?
I bet altogether it smells like, maybe, flowers.

Kia Harris (10)
Abington High School, Wigston

Happiness

Happiness is a touch of breezy blue sky
It is a boast of glittering joy
Happiness is a fizzy sweet that makes you pull funny faces
Happiness is a playful kitten pouncing for its toy
Happiness is a smooth, delightful ice cream with a bright red cherry
on top
Happiness is the scent of sweet lavender on a hot summer's day
Happiness is the cheerful song from the ice cream van
Happiness is a gleaming strawberry waiting to be bitten and explode
with juice.

Melissa Beattie (10)
Abington High School, Wigston

It Feels Like This

Sadness feels like an ocean of blue tears.
Sadness sounds like a lullaby that was sung to my great grandma
who has passed away.
Sadness smells like a pet that you can sense in your house still.
Sadness tastes like the food you have been banned from forever.
Loneliness feels like nobody likes you and that you are invisible.
Anger feels like you could smash a crystal-clear window.
Love feels like a bride wearing a really beautiful dress in a lovely
wedding church.

Rebecca Smith (10)
Abington High School, Wigston

My Feelings Poem!

The sound of happiness is already complete,
The look of surprise is under our feet.
The taste of fear has just arrived,
And the feel of the breeze rushes through your eyes.

The bravery of love is coming by,
The hope of curiosity is going to die.
The sound of love is going to lie,
But for now it's a bye-bye.

Hannah Everton (10)
Abington High School, Wigston

Bravery

The biggest mystery of the world is being brave.
No one can gain it, no one can touch it,
No one can smell it, or even bear it.
You just need to believe in yourself.
The biggest mystery is being brave.

Hannah Cowley (10)
Abington High School, Wigston

Curiosity

Oh curiosity, smells like trouble.
Oh curiosity, sometimes double.
Oh curiosity, so strange and wonderful.
Oh curiosity, just one peep.
Oh curiosity, my footsteps are getting deep.
Oh curiosity, you're no fun.
Now I've just got a smack from Mum!

> *Ouch!*

Jamal Cover (10)
Abington High School, Wigston

I Like The Sight

I like the sight of my mum's shining eye,
I like the sight of my mum's steaming pie,
I like the sight of my guinea pig's play,
I wish that would be me some day.

I like the sight of the clock at 3:05
Although I don't like the enormous beehive,
I like the sight of mince, mash and peas,
I love having it but only for teas.

Katie Bown (10)
Abington High School, Wigston

Excitement

Excitement is luminous green, bright and happy,
Excitement is the sound of people screaming.
Excitement makes all animals happy around the world,
Excitement makes children wound up and ready to go.
Excitement is all in the world, it makes people alive,
Excitement makes children and parents jump up and down.
Excitement is like lemonade running up and down your nose.

Reanne Hipwell (10)
Abington High School, Wigston

Fear

Fear is fiery red.
The mean roar of a lion.
A killer shark coming after you.
A cave, dark, silent, all alone.
A sharp cut of glass.
A scratch along a hard table.
A bad thumping, shaking the ground.
Many sounds you can't imagine.

Megan Ricketts (10)
Abington High School, Wigston

Fear

Fear is a feeling you cannot see,
but it affects both you and me.
It can turn your legs to jelly,
and give you pains in your belly.
It can make you run a mile,
but you should beat it with a smile.
Your mouth will feel ever so dry,
it'll make you not want to try.

Joshua Hartley (11)
Abington High School, Wigston

Happiness

Happiness is a bright yellow,
It's joyful and great,
It's like swimming in chocolate,
It's like stroking a soft dog,
It's the sweet and sour scent of a sweet,
It's running through rainy flowers
And jumping in the warm swimming baths,
Happiness is a glittering rainbow.

Joseph Spencer (10)
Abington High School, Wigston

Fear

Fear is a damson - red, dark and deep
Fear is a misty Amazon of rain
With scary noises within the darkness
Fear is red-hot fire sauce burning in your mouth
Fear is a volcano erupting in Hell with a shower of rock
Fear is chilli pizza with peppers
Fear is never-ending pain, always be afraid!

Jake Edwards (10)
Abington High School, Wigston

Love

Love is the colour of a beating heart.
It looks like hugs and kisses.
It smells like Valentine chocolate.
It tastes like joy and happiness.
It sounds like wedding bells ringing in the distance.

Libby Kennett (10)
Abington High School, Wigston

A Perfect Place

I am walking in the forest,
Where I hear calming sounds of nature,
I go past little fluffy rabbits,
With a little fluffy ball on their bottoms,
I pass little waddling ducks,
With big webbed feet,
I see happy chirping birds,
Flying through the lofty trees,
I feel the fresh air blowing on my face.
The forest is such a perfect place.

Liberty Olivia Lee (8)
Arnold View Primary & Nursery School, Arnold

The Horse

Their unshod hooves thundered across the plains.
The stallions fought with feet and teeth.
A mother's shrill whinny echoed through the mountains.
The wild fire that burned in their souls is dimmed
And memories faded . . .

The plains are bare of them, the stallions fight no more
And no more foals hide in secret glades.
They stand to attention as the saddle is fitted.
They do not flinch as their rider mounts.
They submit to their rider and are commanded.
They obey.
Can't fight.
Don't fight.
Won't fight.

The horse!

Rebekah Anne Foster (10)
Arnold View Primary & Nursery School, Arnold

From An Aeroplane Window

Little patches of fields and houses down below.
Birds flapping their wings at my window!
Other zooming aeroplanes whizzing away miles from ours.
Little tiny dots moving around and about.
Fluffy white clouds floating around.
The crashing sea under my feet.
Little tiny lights from town, buildings twinkling brightly.
Twinkling stars winking at me!
The lights going off in the zooming plane next to ours.
The dazzling moon following the plane.
The whizzing planes landing at the airport before ours.
Dazzling restaurant lights as our plane comes down
As we get closer to the airport.

Simran Dosanjh (9)
Arnold View Primary & Nursery School, Arnold

My Dog Cooper

My dog's called Cooper
He's like a little trooper

My dog Cooper
He's chewed my favourite teddy bear
But he doesn't care

My dog Cooper
He eats everything in the house
He chases my pet mouse

My dog Cooper
He chases butterflies too
Cats, bats and flies to name but a few

My dog Cooper
He isn't house-trained yet
And he won't be in a million years, I bet!

Emily Meadowcroft (9)
Arnold View Primary & Nursery School, Arnold

The Leprechauns

The rainbow, it shines and sparkles.
The pot of gold, it glimmers and gleams.
The leprechauns dance and sing.
They are magical mischief-makers.
They dance and dance all night long.
They never sleep, they are always protecting
their magical, most marvellous, pot of *gold!*

Annette Sandeman (8)
Arnold View Primary & Nursery School, Arnold

Pirate - Acrostic

P arrots on my shoulder
I love valuable gold
R oger is the name of my ship
A red ruby
T reasure in the hold
E xtremely valued gold!

Harman Dosanjh
Arnold View Primary & Nursery School, Arnold

Butterfly, Butterfly

Butterfly, butterfly, fly in the sky.
Butterfly, butterfly, way up high.
Butterfly, butterfly, colourful and bright.
Butterfly, butterfly, landing all around.
Butterfly, butterfly, you shine like the sun.
Butterfly, butterfly gracefully dies.

Emily King (8)
Arnold View Primary & Nursery School, Arnold

Animals

Giraffes are tall
Ants are small
Cheetahs are fast
Turtles are slow
It doesn't matter
They are all special.

Emily-Jane Walker (9)
Arnold View Primary & Nursery School, Arnold

Snow

Snow is sparkling all around
Snowflakes are falling to the ground
Snow makes everything look nice
We can build a snowman with a happy face
But soon the shiny snow turns to ice.

Rhiannon Gordon (7)
Arnold View Primary & Nursery School, Arnold

Autumn Colours

Red, yellow, orange and green
These are the colours that I have seen
On my autumn walk as I stride
The noise of the leaves crackling under my feet
And the birds tweeting with the beat.

Although there are such things I like
There is something that fills me with delight
The pink sunset and the night
But at Hallowe'en we all get a fright
So when I go to bed tonight
I will snuggle up really tight.

Jasmine Rea (8)
Awsworth Primary School, Awsworth

Animals

Animals, big and small
Animals, stripy and tall
Some are nasty, some are mean
Some are never seen
Some hide up in the sky so they can see all of the ground
Especially in the playground.

Grace Gilder-Welch (8)
Awsworth Primary School, Awsworth

My Cat

My cat is fat, white and black
Her favourite place is on a Bugs Bunny mat
She once caught a mouse and left it outside the house
She is partial to the odd wood louse
Her meat is smelly but it fills her belly
Her best dish is a plate of fish
She scratches the sofa and the walls
And pulls the paper off in the hall
My dad says he hates her but it's not true
But whose lap does she always sleep on?
Can you guess who?

Ruby Breward (9)
Awsworth Primary School, Awsworth

Anger

Anger is red like
A hot summer's day.

Anger smells like
A sniff of sadness,
Like a cold winter's night.

Anger sounds like
A piece of badness
From the past.

Anger tastes like
Poisoned food from a witch.

Anger feels like
A piece of my heart breaking.

Anger reminds me of when I was little
And I got picked on.

Joshua Dent (8)
Barnby Road Primary School, Newark

Pain

Pain is red,
As red as the reddest blood.
Pain is black,
As black as an evil king.
Pain is red.

Pain smells of poison,
Like a poisoned apple.
Pain smells like rotting meat,
Like a decaying dinosaur.
Pain smells horrid.

Pain sounds like screeching,
When an owl is hunting in the night.
Pain sounds like the teacher,
When someone's been naughty.
Pain sounds evil.

Pain tastes like mushrooms,
The rawest ever mushrooms.
Pain tastes like fire,
The biggest ever forest fire.
Pain tastes like suncream.

Pain looks like fear,
As fearsome as the biggest lion.
Pain looks like sadness,
As sad as the hungriest giant.
Pain is horrific.

Pain feels like a bone,
A very broken bone.
Pain feels like a saw,
A saw cutting wood.
Pain feels like a paper cut, *Ouch*!

Pain reminds me of wars,
Like a league of super evil.
I haven't got an injury!

Lydia Brailsford
Barnby Road Primary School, Newark

Fun

What colour is it?
Fun is yellow like rich, creamy honey.
Fun is blue like an American sky.
Fun is orange like the beautiful sun.

What does it smell of?
Fun smells of fresh beautiful air.
Fun smells of beautiful summer grass.
Fun smells like fresh water.
Fun smells like children in summer.

What does it sound like?
Fun sounds like a calm day.
Fun sounds like a skipping rope.
Fun sounds like a group of friends playing tig.

What does it taste like?
Fun tastes like hot summer air.
Fun tastes like everyone's breath when they laugh.
Fun tastes like girls' and boys' sweat.
Fun tastes like grazed knees.

What does it look like?
Fun looks like friends skipping happily.
Fun looks like no one is falling out.
Fun looks like everyone is happy.
Fun looks like no one is upset.

What does it feel like?
Fun feels like sweat running down my face.
Fun feels like laughter.
Fun feels like peace.
Fun feels like happiness.

What does it remind you of?
Fun reminds me of summer nights.
Fun reminds me of Christmas Day.
Fun reminds me of wonderful holidays.
Fun reminds me of playing in the snow at Christmas.

Amy Freshney (9)
Barnby Road Primary School, Newark

Fear

Fear is black
Like the midnight sky
Fear is red
Like blood
Fear is white
Like the moon at dark

Fear smells of a rotting egg
I'm going to be sick
Fear smells of mouldy fruit
Like a worm has just wriggled through

Fear sounds like a howling wolf
About to pounce
Fear sounds like fresh blood
Dripping off a hand

Fear tastes like poison
Just given to a human
Fear tastes like dead dog
Very fresh

Fear looks like a full moon
Just going down
Fear looks like a murderer
Just about to kill

Fear feels rock hard
Fear feels stiff
With achy bones

It reminds me of killers
With knives.

Blake Theokritoff (9)
Barnby Road Primary School, Newark

Fun

Fun is red
like a rose.
Fun is yellow
like the stars.

Fun smells like
the air at night.
Fun smells like
the pollen from flowers.

Fun sounds like
the wind hitting against the grass.
Fun sounds like
people laughing together.

Fun tastes like
brown lovely chocolate.
Fun tastes like
red shiny strawberries.

Fun looks like
people laughing.
Fun looks like
people making friends.

Fun feels like
people getting along.
Fun feels like
a rainbow inside you.

Harry Hopkinson (9)
Barnby Road Primary School, Newark

Anger

Anger is red,
Like flames from a fire,
It's what I desire.

Anger smells of spit,
Coming from the mean,
The mean who are not clean.

Anger sounds like a scream,
From the ghost Florence,
My mother went to Torrence.

Anger tastes like chilli,
Pouring down your throat,
It stings more than a fur coat.

Anger is ugly,
With wrinkles everywhere,
If I were you, I would take care.

Anger feels like bones,
All crusty and white,
They squeeze me tight.

Anger reminds me of tigers,
Looking for their prey,
I wouldn't stay.

Grace McKeon (8)
Barnby Road Primary School, Newark

Love

Love is white like . . .
Love is white like . . .
Love is white like snow.

Love smells like . . .
Love smells like . . .
Love smells like roses, red and nice.

Laurie Town (8)
Barnby Road Primary School, Newark

Fun

Fun is yellow like a happy, sunny day,
Fun is blue like the bright sky,
Fun is green like a soft meadow.

Fun smells of party food at the party,
Fun smells of adventure just waiting to happen,
Fun smells of action on the ride.

Fun sounds like screams as the roller coaster dips,
Fun sounds like the dance music in the club,
Fun sounds like the tap of shoes dancing to music.

Fun tastes like the pizza in my mouth,
Fun tastes like birthday cake,
Fun tastes like chips after a great day.

Fun looks like the big roller coaster,
Fun looks like the theme park,
Fun looks like a bright, sunny day.

Fun feels like the whoosh of air from the roller coaster,
Fun feels like the ice cream melting in the sun,
Fun feels like the taps of my feet on the dance floor.

Fun reminds me of great days out,
Fun reminds me of fabulous nights,
Fun reminds me of friends and family.

Luke Wells (9)
Barnby Road Primary School, Newark

Sadness

What colour is it?
Sadness is black
Like a dark bedroom at night.
What does it smell of?
Sadness smells like death
The death of a family member or friend.
What does it sound like?
Sadness sounds like silence
On a dark, cold night.
What does it taste like?
Sadness tastes very tangy like bitter lemon,
What does it look like?
Smeary and murky
Like eyes full of tears.
What does it feel like?
Sadness feels like wind
With drizzle in it.
What does it remind you of?
Sadness reminds me of death
Like when my grandad died.

Abigail Roberts (9)
Barnby Road Primary School, Newark

Happiness

Happiness is as bright as light.
Happiness is not bold but it is gold.
Happiness smells like the sweetest smell ever.
Happiness sounds like true nature.
Happiness sounds like peace.
Happiness tastes like the sweetest smell ever.
Happiness tastes like the yellowest daffodil.
It looks like the brightest treasure.
Happiness feels like the best feeling ever.
Happiness reminds me of the bright sky.

Nathan Scott (8)
Barnby Road Primary School, Newark

Anger

Anger is red like blood and violence
Anger is black like darkness
Anger is blue like tears
Anger smells salty like cries of sadness
Anger smells like bricks, like destruction
Anger smells alcoholic like heavy rock festivals
Anger sounds like screams of pain
Anger sounds like the thunder of boulders tumbling
Anger sounds like 4000 stomps in Hell
Anger tastes of blood spilt from fights
Anger tastes of skin when you bite with hate
Anger tastes of poison when you get your own back
Anger is a skeleton when you kill with loathing
Anger is death when it comes late at night
Anger is a body found in a car
Anger feels cold and bitter, driving you insane
Anger feels apocalyptic constantly taking you to the edge
Anger feels like a sword jabbing you in the head
Anger reminds you of heavy, loud rock music out of control
Anger reminds you of revenge and madness.

Jacob Ketley (10)
Barnby Road Primary School, Newark

Love

Love is red, which stays in your heart.
Love smells of happiness that travels all around us.
Love sounds like birds tweeting peacefully.
Love sounds like trees waving in the thin air.
Love tastes of sweet, shiny strawberries twinkling in the light.
Love looks like red and pink love hearts glittering in the sky.
Love feels like happiness running inside you.
Love reminds me of the wonderful past.
Love reminds me of the wonder of the future.

Megan Holly Brown (8)
Barnby Road Primary School, Newark

Love

Love is red
Like soft snug heat.
Love smells
Like strength inside you.
Love sounds
Like peace around you.
Love tastes
Like sugar and sweets.
Love looks
Like fluffy clouds in Heaven.
Love feels
Like protection and safety.
Love reminds
Me of happiness.

Indiana-Rose Kayrak (8)
Barnby Road Primary School, Newark

Happiness

Happiness is yellow
like a calm, warm sun.
Happiness smells of laughter and joy
like the wind in the trees.
Happiness sounds like birds singing
in the trees calmly.
Happiness tastes like chocolate mountains
when the birds sing calmly.
Happiness looks like joy and excitement
like the calm sun.
Happiness feels like a dark summer's night
in a warm bath.
Happiness reminds me of my nana who died.

Georgia Lowdon (9)
Barnby Road Primary School, Newark

Sadness

Sadness is a gloomy grey,
Like a dusty chimney.
It smells sooty and old,
Like dusty gold.
It sounds like a long moan,
In an angry tone.
It tastes wet and soggy,
Like a stew that is very boggy.
It looks really grey and misty,
Like the moon.
It feels slimy and old
And very cold.

Lucas Eden (8)
Barnby Road Primary School, Newark

Happiness

Happiness is bright and yellow,
It brightens up your door.
Happiness smells like home,
On a brightened-up day.
Happiness sounds like goodness.
It tastes like lemon,
On a hot summer's day.
Happiness looks like victory
On a bright yellow day.
It feels soft and comfortable.
It reminds me of a good family day.

Tamzin Eaglestone (9)
Barnby Road Primary School, Newark

Fun, Fun, Fun

Fun is like a rainbow with different activities.
Fun is the smell of joy.
Fun sounds like laughter and happiness.
Fun tastes like fresh air and a new day.
Fun looks like roller coasters in a fair.
Fun feels like a great day.
Fun reminds me of joy and happiness.

Fun is in my world, is it in yours?

Courtney Woolley (8)
Barnby Road Primary School, Newark

Anger

Red is like sunburn.
Red is like sunburn on your back.

Anger smells of food being burnt.
Anger sounds like someone being hurt.
Anger tastes of food being ruined.
It looks like someone being murdered.
It feels horrible.
It reminds me of being hurt.

Anikin Watson (9)
Barnby Road Primary School, Newark

Silence

Silence is transparent like the air around us.
Silence smells of fresh dew on the bluebells.
Silence is peaceful and relaxing.
Silence tastes like sweet honey, fresh from the hive.
Silence is as still as ice.
Silence is relaxing and comforts you.
Silence reminds me of the empty classroom at break.

Jasper Cantwell (8)
Barnby Road Primary School, Newark

Fun

Red is a bright morning sunrise.
Happiness is when my friends let me play with them.
Happiness is when people are laughing.
Lots of people play with other people.
It tastes like a nice taste.
It looks happy and fun.
It feels really fun to play with my friends.
It reminds me of my grandma when she comes round.

Adam Ashmore (8)
Barnby Road Primary School, Newark

Anger

Anger is red like the hot boiling lava.
Anger smells like the toilet
When it has not been cleaned for a year.
Anger sounds like two men fighting.
Anger tastes like red-hot peppers boiling in a pan.
Anger feels like madness.
Anger reminds me of my mum and dad play-fighting.

Phoebe Gissing (8)
Barnby Road Primary School, Newark

Surprise

Surprise is red like a present wrapped up and ready to give
Surprise smells of happiness and love
Surprise sounds like music whistling in my ears
Surprise tastes like chocolate fresh from the factory
Surprise looks like a theme park in the distance
Surprise feels like squishy toffee
Surprise reminds me of a lush green summer meadow.

Ruby Bennett
Barnby Road Primary School, Newark

The Teacher Jumped Out Of The Window

The teacher jumped out of the window.
The master rapidly ran for the door.
The nurse and the librarian escaped.
They are not coming back anymore.

Bye-bye!
Have fun, you are not coming home.
The councillor hollering madly,
He escaped out of the gym.
The coach and the man shouted out
And they ran after him.
They're not coming back anymore, no more.

What fun, they ran.
They're not coming back anymore.
The dinner ladies threw up their bags,
The plates from the kitchen cupboard
And all the children looked puzzled.
The member scurried away.
It was pretty cool to see the teachers excited,
To leave school until next year.

Saleha Dadabay
Charnwood Primary School, Leicester

The Rainbow

Once there was a rainbow in the sky
I love rainbows, a rainbow is a beautiful thing
and a bright thing.
The rainbow is red, blue, pink, green, yellow, orange
and the rainbow is the best thing.
When the rainbow is out, I feel happy.

Humairaa Patel (7)
Charnwood Primary School, Leicester

Shoes

I bought some shoes
Nice and gold
I wore them for so long
That they got really old
I wanted a new pair
But my dad said, 'Don't you dare!'
My dad said, 'You can do window shopping
As long as you stop hopping.'
With the money I had I bought a hat
How I wish I could hit my dad with a cricket bat
My dad is the best
And he gave me a test
If I passed the test
I'd become the best
He said it was fair
To buy a new pair
Of those golden shoes
That I always wanted to wear.

Aqeelah Fakir (10)
Charnwood Primary School, Leicester

I'm Late To Go To Sleep

I go to sleep but the alarm clock goes *beep.*
I fall down the stairs,
I land on some chairs.
All I can see is the TV screen.
Now I wonder *where's my tea?*
Without being seen, I go to sleep.
Sometimes I'm lazy
And sometimes I go crazy.
I am tall.
I play football.
I work at the till
Without paying a bill.

Muhammad Diwan (10)
Charnwood Primary School, Leicester

Faces, Faces, Even On Cars

Faces, faces, even on cars
also on delicious chocolate bars
but not usually found on Mars
I also see them in the cars

Faces, faces, neither sweet nor sour
but I don't think they're taller than the Eiffel Tower
they might be really hot or cold
I don't think faces grow mould.

Faces, faces, even on cars
also on delicious chocolate bars
but not usually found on Mars
I also see them in the cars.

Faces, faces, either rude or nice
faces can also eat yummy rice
faces either mean or sweet
but not all faces can tweet.

Kinzah Gulzar (9)
Charnwood Primary School, Leicester

Science Rules!

Support science
Can get you anywhere
Is that the best you can do?
Eat healthy food
Never lets you down
Can help you
Everywhere you go is science!

Run to be healthy
Unhealthy, bad luck for you!
Learn even more
Everywhere you go, science is there
Science rules!

Muhammad Umarmia Patia (10)
Charnwood Primary School, Leicester

36

Morning Blues

I woke up with a yawn
at the crack of dawn
I banged my head
on the side of the bed

I ran down the stairs
and saw a flock of bears
I dropped some milk
on my mum's pure silk

My sister had to train
her big filled brain
and learn her maths
and take a bath

My mum came in her gown
she gasped and looked down
she saw some milk
on her pure, pure silk!

Fatima Mamodohanif (9)
Charnwood Primary School, Leicester

Summer And Spring

S unshine glimmering on a hot summer's day,
U nending queues at the boat bay,
M y body is sweating with heat,
M int-coloured slippers on my feet,
E ating ice cream on warm sands,
R unning up sand dunes seeing many lands.

S quirrels scampering along green grass,
P eople wishing their icy drinks would last,
R ain is never felt,
I f ice was left, it would melt,
N et on windows blowing slightly,
G eese crawling into the pond, splashing lightly.

Aisha Patel (9)
Charnwood Primary School, Leicester

Teachers

My homework is too much,
and I'd rather not touch.
It is never less,
and I always make a mess.

What I have done
was clearly a mistake.
But maybe it is
time for a break.

My teacher comes to school,
and is never a fool.
There are whizzing creatures
which add excellent features.

My teacher is pretty
and is never a pity.
She is so grateful
that it's never regretful.

Hafsah Sheikh (9)
Charnwood Primary School, Leicester

Books

Books and lots of books
even in the library
even in the shops
also you get magazines the same as books
books are everywhere.

Books have pictures
books have writing
and sometimes you find books at your home.

Books don't have good looks
books have pictures which are done by people
books are done by many people.

Khadijah Patel (9)
Charnwood Primary School, Leicester

I Got Up Late For School Today

I got up late for school today,
And nearly missed the bus!
I hurried down the stairs,
Wolfed down my toast and caused a fuss!

I quickly threw books in my bag,
My pens, lunch and shorts,
Grabbed my coat from out the cupboard,
Took my bats and ball for sports.

I slid across the kitchen floor,
And hopped around the cat,
And expertly rolled over,
Jumped back up and grabbed my hat.

I belted out from the front door,
Spun round and swung it shut,
Saw the bus waiting for me,
I felt I had time to strut.

Imran Ghumra (9)
Charnwood Primary School, Leicester

I'm Making A Pizza . . .

I'm making a pizza
that can toss and turn like a frisbee.

I'm making a pizza
that looks like a steering wheel.

I'm making a pizza
that is delectable for a treat.

I'm making a pizza
that is tasty and yummy to eat.

I'm making a pizza
that is lovely for a family.

Abubakar Seedat (9)
Charnwood Primary School, Leicester

The Talking Cat

On my way to school one day
I met a talking cat
She said, 'Hello, how are you?'
And then she stole my precious hat
I said, 'Please give it back.'
Instead she put it in her enormous sack
She said, 'See you later.'
And started to walk towards her house.
I followed behind her
And on the way we met a mouse
The mouse said in a mysterious voice
'How are you?'
I said, 'I'm fine, thank you.'
The mouse turned towards the cat
And said, 'You can eat me if you give the hat back.'
But as she gave me the hat
The clever mouse ran away.

Zainab Saleh (9)
Charnwood Primary School, Leicester

Football Poem

Man U is my best team
my brother supports Tottenham
they lose every match
even against Blackburn.

Whoever Man U versus
I sit down and watch them play
they won the Champions League
and they play nearly every day

Giggs is in Man U
he is a skilful player
his position is midfielder
and also he is a free-kick taker.

Adam Patel (9)
Charnwood Primary School, Leicester

Caught Red-Handed

Giraffes are tall
Some people work at a till
I play football
If I don't I have to pay a bill

Sometimes I'm lazy
Sometimes I go crazy
I like Tic-Tacs
And KitKat

I like movies
That are not groovy
I love dodgeball
And fussball
Sometimes I run
I like bread buns
I like helping
Especially painting.

Saalif Ibrahimo Acharafali (9)
Charnwood Primary School, Leicester

My Sister's Annoying

My sister is annoying
She's always singing
Up in her room
It sounds like a boom!

When she goes to school
She's always acting cool
When she screams
It means she needs a bundle of *ice cream* . .

I need to know why she does all this
I don't know why she says Miss
To my sweet mum
My sister is really very *dumb!*

Sadiyah Nasrulla (9)
Charnwood Primary School, Leicester

41

A True Student

I come daily to school
I use my stationery tools
learning my rules.
A lot of things I have learnt.
without getting burnt.
When I have a fight
I don't bite
but in fact, get out into the light.

I eat my lunch
with a great munch.
I play the game of ball
with my mates who are tall.

I write through the night
which makes me really bright.
I work really hard
in my schoolyard.

Mohammad Abdus Samad (9)
Charnwood Primary School, Leicester

Cricket Is The Best

Cricket is a good sport,
You play with a bat and ball,
It has its own fort,
And if you are careless you might brutally fall.

The bowler bowls,
The crowds roar,
The batter smashes it for four,
And then the ball rolls.

The bowler gets angry and bowls as fast as he can.
The ball shoots like a rocket,
He has all his fans,
The batter misses and the ball hits his ball and socket.

Usman Bhana (9)
Charnwood Primary School, Leicester

The Beach

The day I went to the beach
I came home looking like an orange peach.
I was lying down in the blazing sun,
When my eye caught sight of a massive bun.
I got up to see if it was real
But it was only a little brown seal.

The day I went to the beach
I came home looking like an orange peach.

When I was swimming in the water I saw a coat
I got the red coat and I jumped into the boat.
Somebody was doing backstrokes in the water
I got up to see who it was but it was only my auntie's daughter.

The day I went to the beach
I came home looking like an orange peach.

Amarah Kandawala (9)
Charnwood Primary School, Leicester

Mother Nature

Mother Nature controls nature
Oranges are Mother Nature's favourite fruits, yummy!
Trees are all because of Mother Nature
Happy Hollow is where Mother Nature lives
Everyone knows Mother Nature exists, do you?
River making is one of Mother Nature's talents.

Nature is made by Mother Nature and that's why spring is a very
memorable season.
Apples are made by Mother Nature, especially to keep us healthy
Tomatoes sometimes come out weird shapes
Because it is made to always remember Mother Nature
Umbrellas are made to stop the rain which is made especially to
quench our thirst.

Hafsah Khalifa
Charnwood Primary School, Leicester

I Have A Kitty Named Scruffy

I have a kitty named Scruffy,
She is so fluffy,
She is quite chubby
And likes to sleep on the carpet which is ever so lumpy.

My kitty named Scruffy
Loves this song of mine.

'Kitty-cat, Kitty-cat
How do you do?
Kitty-cat, Kitty-cat
Where are you?
Kitty-cat, Kitty-cat
What to do?
Kitty-cat, Kitty-cat
How do you do?'

Muhibo Abdalla (9)
Charnwood Primary School, Leicester

The Nature

The white fluffy clouds look like candyfloss and are as pure
as a newly washed blanket which is also as clean as you.
And the baby blue attractive sky is as soft as a baby's bottom
and as blue as the waves,
And down on the ground there are different colour combinations
of red, yellow, white, brown, pink and blue flowers
and the blank space is flowers by green grass and leaves.
But when people change their behaviour, so the weather changes
and clouds go grey and it starts to thunder, storm and rain.
Then the people learn their lesson and out comes the rainbow
with colours red, pink, yellow, green and purple.

Ayesha Hussain (9)
Charnwood Primary School, Leicester

Funny Poems

If you want to sleep in my bed,
You must be fed,
If you want to be a nurse,
You must bring a purple purse.
If you have knickers
You must bring me Snickers

Are you clever? OK,
Do you know all about maths?
What's so wrong about having a bath?
I bet you know the right path.

Tasneem Varachhia (9)
Charnwood Primary School, Leicester

Star In The Sky

The star is so bright
In the middle of the night
As it twinkles in the sky

I cannot deny
That it isn't very big
It's just so far away

I could lie under the moon
Watching the stars twinkle in the sky

My, oh my, what a wonderful sight
If only I could come with them

I wish they could take me to Jupiter
And fly me round the moon
And see the Earth from a height.

But I guess that will never happen
So I better dream, dream, dream.

Monica Spear (10)
Chuter Ede Primary School, Newark

My School

I go to school,
Almost every day of my life,
It's not worth it,
As the elves in the office give me detention,
If I turn up 10 seconds late.
The dragons in my classroom don't teach,
They just tell us what to do,
While drinking cold lava,
The head teacher's the worst,
He prances around in a tutu in assembly,
And embarrasses us when important people come to the school,
I can't tell you what he does,
It's just too rude,
Thinking about it, the trolls are worse,
They serve glop and gloop for lunch and try to pass it as food, *yuck!*
My witch and wizard parents don't care about it,
Got to go, the gnomes are coming!

Emma Parkin (11)
Chuter Ede Primary School, Newark

Questionology

'Take my lesson in questionology,'
Said Mr Gugg in science.
'Asking things is easy and fun,
We do it all the time.
England, France, everywhere,
Curiosity can flow.
Knowledge came from asking,
and that's why I am here.
I don't have every answer,
But I'm happy to help.
Just before you go,
Homework's due tomorrow,
Bye-bye, ta-ta for now!'

Katie-Jane Clancy (10)
Chuter Ede Primary School, Newark

Anger

Anger stomped over to a barn house,
A cheery man was whistling while cleaning out a horse stable,
Seeing happy people made Anger even madder,
He cast a ghostly,
The horse went mad,
It kicked and spat,
The man and stable were a mess.

Anger left the stable a wreck,
The man had stopped whistling,
Anger had got what he wanted,
Then stormed off to go and find someone else to make miserable,
He did find a few kids but picked the nicest and happiest one.

Abbie Thompson (10)
Chuter Ede Primary School, Newark

Jazz

A dog is just a pet for me,
My dog is sweet, loving, *wondrous,*
She's old and not very lively at all,
People say she must be *precious,*
If dogs like walks, why doesn't she?
She must be extremely *luxurious,*
Now she has grey hairs on top,
I hope she isn't *poisonous,*
Some dogs are really big,
Not her, she is just *gorgeous,*
You would never see her run so fast,
Honestly it would be *preposterous!*

Ashleigh Bowles (10)
Chuter Ede Primary School, Newark

Me!

Everyone thought I was a cat,
When I helped eat the kitchen rat,
Everyone thought I was a dog,
When I started licking people at playtime,
Everyone thought I was a rabbit
When they saw my lunch, a whole lot of carrots,
Everyone thought I was a bird,
When I flew to school, not taking the bus,
But really I'm just me,
A very talented jumbly.

Ruth Jackson (9)
Chuter Ede Primary School, Newark

Pirates · Acrostic

P irates sail the seven seas
I n search of land and gold
R emember, they own the seven seas
A nd if you ever see them, your money you should hold
'T reasure! Land ahoy!' They bellow from the seven seas
E ver ferocious, strong and bold
S earch you may, the seven seas . . . to behold!

Chloe Wisbey (9
Chuter Ede Primary School, Newark

The Snow

The snow has fallen and now the sky is blue.
Tree branches are heavy and icicles hang trembling.
Snow crunches as people walk through
Leaving their deep footprints behind.
The pond has been frozen by the sparkling, dazzling ice.
The snow is melting by the blazing hot sun.

Kathryn Anne Lee (8)
Chuter Ede Primary School, Newark

Fun

Fun is multicoloured in the rainbow out of the sky.
Fun is the smell of dark chocolate like flowers.
Fun is the sound of big bangs of drums.
Fun is the taste of apples inside with juice.
Fun is the look of people laughing with joy.
Fun feels like balls hitting you on your hand playing catch.
Fun reminds me of my friend laughing at the park.

Owen Riley (9)
Cloudside Junior School, Sandiacre

Fun

The colour of fun is multicoloured.
The smell of fun is red roses.
The sound of fun is birds tweeting in the sky.
It tastes like a doughnut.
It looks like a playful playground.
It feels like a happy feeling.
It reminds me of a sun.

Brandon Edwards-Timms (9)
Cloudside Junior School, Sandiacre

Power

Power is red like lava going over the top of a volcano.
It smells like the blood of a warrior,
It tastes like a cold polar bear.
It sounds like an eagle's prey.
It looks like a god from out of the sky.
It feels like a bullet into my thigh.
It reminds me of Dad picking me up for the first time.

Tom Rigby (9)
Cloudside Junior School, Sandiacre

Pride

Pride reminds me of a man
fighting a lion with his bare hands.

Pride feels like you're important
and it makes you feel good.

Pride is orange like a satsuma.
Pride smells like a satsuma being peeled.

Joe Stoppiello (9)
Cloudside Junior School, Sandiacre

Happiness

Happiness is multicoloured, like flashing rainbows all over the world.
Happiness reminds me of everybody in the world just having fun.
Happiness smells of big bursting flowers on a windy summer's day.
Happiness looks like smiley faces around the world.
Happiness tastes like children sharing their deep, dark chocolate.
Happiness feels like a big bowl of softness on a winter's day.

Ellie Edwards (9)
Cloudside Junior School, Sandiacre

Terror

Terror is red like a heart beating at a slow pace.
Terror smells like the blood of someone who has been killed.
Terror looks like a bullet that's come through a baby.
Terror feels like wet, cold blood.
Terror reminds me of part of my family that passed away.

Scott Toplis (9)
Cloudside Junior School, Sandiacre

50

Love

Love is like loads of pink shiny shoes.
Love looks like a beautiful pink flamingo in the air.
Love is like eating a pink chocolate cake.
Love is like drinking a fluffy pink milkshake.
Love is like a family hugging each other.

Shannon Beadsworth (9)
Cloudside Junior School, Sandiacre

Kelly

K is for Kelly, that is me!
E is for eager as can be.
L is for laughs with everyone.
L is for looks out for fun.
Y is for young, yes, that's me!

Kelly Goddard (9)
Cloudside Junior School, Sandiacre

My Birthday

On my birthday sitting in bed
The big day arrived with lots to be said!
Yesterday when I lost my tooth
I got £10, and that's the truth!
At 8.30, I opened my presents
Ben 10 Omnitrix and 2 toy pheasants!
A digger set and a very tall sign
On the Wii I got F1 2009!
At 9.00 the post came
He gave me a slingshot with great aim!
The next parcel was a drawing pad
The label said 'from Alex and Chad'!
In bed I said, 'Goodnight Mom and Dad'
I settled down to sleep in bed!

Joe Molineaux (7)
Cropwell Bishop Primary School, Cropwell Bishop

Light Vs Dark

Light is bright
Light is pale,
Dark is old
Dark is stale.

Light is shining
Light is full,
Dark is aged
Dark is dull.

Light is awesome
Light is great,
Dark is scary
Dark is hate.

Light is happy
Light is glad,
Dark is frightful
Dark is mad.

Light is cool
Light is cheerful,
Dark is horrible
Dark is tearful.

George Clark (10)
Cropwell Bishop Primary School, Cropwell Bishop

What Is The Moon?

The moon is a car wheel
spinning round and round.
It is a silver medal on my chest
shining proudly.
It is an end of a spoon
feeding endless space.
The moon is a metal tooth
eating the stars.

Oliver Barlow (9)
Cropwell Bishop Primary School, Cropwell Bishop

Autumn Mornings

I opened the willow curtains one autumn morning.
I saw dew on the grass and mist in the distance.
The light had changed without me noticing from shadowy to bright.
I heard birds chirping while lawnmowers chattered in the distance.

I watched squirrels prancing to hazelnuts which prickled under my feet.
I gazed up through the weaving, curved branches of a beech tree.
Some leaves smelt almost like apple juice.
Others looked as if they'd been dipped in deep red wine.

This morning arrived and I opened the willow curtains once again.
Today I saw no dew on the grass and no mist.
Instead I saw a queue of poplar trees looking almost like skyscrapers.
So tall, they looked like they were showing off.
Intelligent and wise they were, stretching up to grab the clouds.

I picked an autumn-coloured apple, red, orange, yellow and green as can be.
I ran back into the willow tree without anyone noticing me.
I hugged its trunk and found a crocodile carved in the rough bark.

Lydia Bulmer (8)
Cropwell Bishop Primary School, Cropwell Bishop

What Are . . . Stars?

Stars are a child's picture
Hanging on their bedroom wall.
They're a Christmas decoration
standing proudly at the top of the tree.
They're fireworks exploding in the sky.
They're lights in the garden
Shining as the sun sets.
They make pictures in the sky
That people can draw.

Louis Molineaux (9)
Cropwell Bishop Primary School, Cropwell Bishop

What Is Mist?

Mist is the steam that comes out of a kettle
that dances happily in the air.

It is grey cloud howling past to fight back with the sun
and cover her with all eternity.

Mist is eerie, hiding creatures from our sight,
making it hard to find our way.

It is a grey crackled leaf floating and drifting
in different directions.

It is free from gravity and walking on the ground
is no such thing.

Leah Halford (9)
Cropwell Bishop Primary School, Cropwell Bishop

What Is The Moon?

The moon is a CD,
it is nice and dark.

The moon is a disco ball,
shining as it hangs from the roof.

The moon is light,
the light is shining in the dark.

The moon is a coin,
glistening on space's floor.

The moon is a metal pan,
it is large and round.

Aidan Wardle (9)
Cropwell Bishop Primary School, Cropwell Bishop

What Are . . . Stars?

The stars are mini disco balls
shining in the darkness of my room.

They are silver coins dangling in the sky
for everyone to see.

They are pearls of a necklace
falling from night's broken chain.

They are ghosts hovering in the moonlight
brightening the world atmosphere.

They are glowing dragon scales
shining in the night sky.

George Barlow (10)
Cropwell Bishop Primary School, Cropwell Bishop

What Are Stars?

The stars are small diamonds in the midnight sky
shining brightly.

They are pieces of silver fluff hanging in the sky,
it's victory for people to see.

The stars are gigantic disco balls
glinting in the colours of light.

The stars are silver medals
glinting on a post ready to be worn.

The stars are CDs as big as beach balls
ready to be played and spun like a cartwheel.

Eleanor Herrington (9)
Cropwell Bishop Primary School, Cropwell Bishop

What Are . . . Stars?

Stars are tiny golden medals floating in the sky,
Shining down for everyone to see.

They are Rice Krispies,
Thrown up into the air.

They are flakes of blossom,
Spinning softly up there shining down to everyone.

They are round pieces of sweetcorn,
Scattered gently from Heaven, falling softly here and there.

They are flecks of yellow paint,
Splattered on a sheet of pale blue paper.

Annalise Armstrong (9)
Cropwell Bishop Primary School, Cropwell Bishop

Stars

Stars are silver disco balls
hanging on my bedroom wall for all to see.

They are silver pearls
shining brightly in the sky as midnight comes.

They are silver coins
spilling from a midnight purse.

They are bike bells ringing and dinging
in the dark black midnight sky.

They are small silver diamonds
falling from the sky for everyone to see.

Kate Elkington (9)
Cropwell Bishop Primary School, Cropwell Bishop

Lightning

Lightning is a laser coming from an alien spaceship
   zooming around in the midnight sky.
It is a sheet of golden paper
   falling down from space.
It is a disco ball on the roof
   swinging from side to side.
Lightning is an aeroplane flying up high
   soaring in the darkness.
It is a siren from a police car
   driving down the lane.

Samuel Jones (9)
Cropwell Bishop Primary School, Cropwell Bishop

Winter

Winter comes with a sparkle of snow,
Down come the snowflakes, *ho, ho, ho!*
Here comes someone on their sledge,
There's some snow on the window ledge.
I hope I see some stars tonight,
I can see the Christmas lights.
Snowballs on the ground,
To see Santa, it's over a pound.
I can hear bells,
And that mince pie smells.

Lucy McLean (8)
Cropwell Bishop Primary School, Cropwell Bishop

Dark · Acrostic

D arkness is here.
A ghost shrieks.
R ats scurry along.
K ing of darkness is here.

Alex Johnson (10)
Cropwell Bishop Primary School, Cropwell Bishop

57

Clouds

The cloud is a sheep
that is floating in mid-air.
It is a piece of cotton wool
stuck on a piece of blue paper.
It is a piece of chewing gum
stuck on the sun.
It is a marshmallow
kicked high into a summer's sky.
It's a blob of white paint
that's been squeezed on the sky.

Lauren Banks (9)
Cropwell Bishop Primary School, Cropwell Bishop

Stars All Over

The stars are little stones
gleaming and shining.
They are silver leaves
falling from a Heavenly tree.
They are silver rubbers
sitting in the shadow of a pencil.
They are sparks splattered all over
lighting up the night sky.
They are silver coins
spread through the dark wallet.

Joseph Blackmore (9)
Cropwell Bishop Primary School, Cropwell Bishop

What Am I?

Fast runner
Meat eater
Fearsome fighter
Silent predator
Loud roarer
Deep sleeper

What am I?
A: Lion.

Owen Lucas (8)
Cropwell Bishop Primary School, Cropwell Bishop

Winter

Winter springs like a song,
merrily, merrily along.
By day they sleep with glorious dreams.
The sunshine rises with a melting scene,
people go out touching the floor with a shining sky.
People miss winter with a glorious song
with merrily, merrily along
but never forget the glowing star tonight.

Nakeisha Creed (8)
Cropwell Bishop Primary School, Cropwell Bishop

Owl

Head turner
Silent flyer
Mouse catcher
Day sleeper
Night hunter
Loud hooter
Tree rooster.

Jaime-Leigh Lucas (7)
Cropwell Bishop Primary School, Cropwell Bishop

59

Stars

Stars are silver buttons on a silky blue blouse,
hanging on night's gloomy rail.
They are pearly white teeth,
chomping in a dark mouth.
They are pearly quartz buried in thick darkness,
reflecting light, floating temptingly.

Katie Elliott (9)
Cropwell Bishop Primary School, Cropwell Bishop

What Is Snow?

Snow is feathers falling from the sky.
It is white pom-poms dancing in the air.
It is cotton wool all over the floor.
It is white baubles hanging from the clouds.
It is white pastry dropping from a giant's pie.

Clarke Dabell (10)
Cropwell Bishop Primary School, Cropwell Bishop

Ghost ·Acrostic

G o, go, the ghost is near
H ide. hide, we're full of fear
O *oooo! Oooo!* shrieks the ghoul
S cream, scream, it's Halloween
T rick or treat?

Abigail McGeachie (8)
Cropwell Bishop Primary School, Cropwell Bishop

Spider's Monologue

Cats, birds, dogs, snakes and those horrifying humans,
you name, it, they all prey on me.
Birds mostly prey on me, and those stupid snakes
are fond of my skin.
My body is a bomb, as round as a cylinder.
I am as scary as Scary Mary.
My job is to spin webs and catch flies for my young.
I love it when the lovely flies tickle my tongue.
I love being a spider because I can get into small spaces,
because my body changes shape.
Can you squeeze into small spaces?
But when you find me, I am only the size of a pea,
so please don't hurt me.

Kerrie McCann (9)
Eastlands Junior School, Meden Vale

The Spider's Monologue

Cats and birds prey on me, and snakes are fond of my skin.
My body is a bomb, as round as a cylinder
and I have long, loose legs.
My job is to make webs and catch flies for my young,
the flies tickle the end of my tongue.
I love being a spider, it is as sweet as a plum,
I can squeeze into small gaps and hide.
Would you like to hide sometime?
Come down into the gaps and have tea with me and laugh all night.
So when you find me, I'm only the size of a pea,
so please don't hurt me.
I don't bite or anything horrible, I'm very friendly.

Joseph French (9)
Eastlands Junior School, Meden Vale

What Bugs Me

When my brother breaks something.
When my sister shouts at my mum.
When my mum shouts at me.
When my dad threatens to burp in my face.
When my sister sleeps with me when I say no.
When my mum tells me I need to do my hideous homework.
When my teacher shouts at Josh.
When my mum tells me to do my room.
What bugs me most is when my dad snores and I cannot get to
sleep.

Megan Wilkinson (9)
Eastlands Junior School, Meden Vale

The Spider's Monologue

Cats, dogs, snakes and those horrifying humans,
you name it, they all prey on me.
I look like a predator, but I'm harmless,
my long legs swish past window ledges.
I like to catch fat, juicy flies, I like to spin silver webs.
I love being a spider but I just don't want to die,
being a spider is a very, very hard job,
you don't get to go to sleep.
But when you find me, don't hurt me,
because I'm only the size of a pea.

Callan Smith (9)
Eastlands Junior School, Meden Vale

What Bugs Me

When I've got to go to bed
What bugs me
When I've got to do what my mum said
What bugs me
When I'm not allowed to play
What bugs me
When I'm at school all day
What bugs me
When I get told off all the time.

Sam Parkin (10)
Eastlands Junior School, Meden Vale

A Spider's Monologue

Cats, dogs, snakes and those hideous humans,
you name it, they all prey on me.
Fish are fond of my flesh.
I'm just a small, eight-eyed arachnid,
I wish I was a butterfly but no, I'm a stupid, old spider.
But I'm not that bad, I get rid of flies for you,
but you continue to trap me in a cup.
Oh well, that's just my luck!

Luke Knight (9)
Eastlands Junior School, Meden Vale

Spider's Monologue

Cats, dogs, snakes and those horrifying humans,
you name it, they all prey on me.
I look like a Coco Pop, my legs are long and thin.
I spin a shiny silver web for my bed.
If you like spiders, webs and flies,
you can be my best friend because I am lonely.
I wish I was a beautiful butterfly so I could escape to the sky.

Charlie Ward (9)
Eastlands Junior School, Meden Vale

What Bugs Me

When my uncle plays my drums.
When I have to get up for school.
When my teacher tells me off.
When I have to do homework.
When my dog wakes me up.
When I have to do miserable maths.
When my friends kick me in football.
What bugs me the most is when my TV doesn't work.

Corey Pullin (9)
Eastlands Junior School, Meden Vale

Autumn Poem

The bright orange, red and yellow leaves crunch and crumple under your cold feet.
Twigs snap, crunch under the Robin Hood tree.
Twigs snap while you are running through them.
The stars are as white a sheep sparkling past your window.
The moon is as bright as a diamond.
Fireworks pop, crackle and sparkle.

Chanel Paige Gibson (9)
Eastlands Junior School, Meden Vale

What Bugs Me

When my brother kisses me.
When my brother jumps on me.
When my mum gets me up and I am tired.
When my brother plays Ben 10 on the Wii.
When I get sent to bed.
When my auntie cuddles me.
When my mum doesn't give me any sweets.

Poppy Lee Shaw (9)
Eastlands Junior School, Meden Vale

Autumn Poem

The cold autumn wind against my face.
The crispy brown leaves fall to the ground.
Auntie Marlene's bonfire, burgers, hot dogs, mushy peas
and jacket potatoes.
Catherine wheels go round - watch the sparkler,
it might burn me!

Jamie Plews (9)
Eastlands Junior School, Meden Vale

The Autumn Poem

The moon is a white warrior fighting the night sky.
Bonfires are a light bulb lighting up the room.
The leaves are falling off the tree like the corn gets harvested.
Bonfires crackle like leaves under my feet.
Bubbling bacon spitting in the frying pan.
Leaves are a chameleon.

Damian Kevin May (9)
Eastlands Junior School, Meden Vale

Ponies

Ponies canter all day long,
in the rain, fog and sun.
It's such a joy to see them
playing, jumping, rolling, having fun.
I pass the field and they stare at me,
with a knowing look - *you're a friend to me.*

Brogan Shaw (11)
Eastlands Junior School, Meden Vale

The Spider Escape

Cats, dogs, snakes and mostly monstrous humans,
they stomp, chomp, whack and smack.
I'm fat, round and hairy.
I spin my sticky, silky web to catch my frightened flies.
But I love who I am, a 4-eyed, 8-legged spider,
I love my body and I wouldn't want to change.

Abbie Deakin (9)
Eastlands Junior School, Meden Vale

The Spider's Monologue

Cats, dogs, snakes and those humans,
you name it, they all prey on me.
I'm as hairy as a monkey
with light, lovely, long legs.
I love to spin webs because it is my job.
I catch juicy flies for my famished family.

Ricky Nathan Alan Lack (9)
Eastlands Junior School, Meden Vale

Spider's Monologue

Cats, dogs, lizards and the horrific humans, they all prey on me.
I'm ugly but I'm proud.
My job is spinning webs and catching flies.
I don't like being a spider because I get killed by a paper.
I may not have it all but neither do you.

Elle Smalley (9)
Eastlands Junior School, Meden Vale

Angry

What does it smell like?
Anger is a smell of burning fire.

What does it sound like?
Anger is like a bull running to you.

What does it remind you of?
Anger reminds you of lightning.

What colour is it?
It is a burning red, like fire.

What does it look like?
Anger is when someone's face is bright red.

What does it taste like?
Anger tastes like a lemon in your mouth.

What does it feel like?
A bomb exploding inside you.

Georgia Duvel (7)
Leen Mills Primary School, Hucknall

Love Heart

Love is the sun rising, the sun crashing,
the stars disappearing.

Love is the sound of the church choir
singing 'Hallelujah' as you get married.

Love is a picnic beside the biggest waterfall
in the world.

Love is a first kiss, just struck midnight.

Love is the feeling of no gravity,
the feeling of us sinking.

Love is red, like a healthy beating heart.
But be careful, the healthy heart can break!

Eleanor Louise Gladman (11)
Leen Mills Primary School, Hucknall

Smile!

Happiness is the yellow of a euphoric face
with a big, bright smile.

Happiness is the giggle of a happy toddler.

Happiness looks like a floral garden
in full bloom.

Happiness moves like children
unwrapping their first ever presents.

Happiness reminds us of a dark room
full of smiling faces.

Happiness feels like an autumn breeze,
soft but firm.

Happiness is like the taste of snow-white
ice cream.

Ellie Batey (11)
Leen Mills Primary School, Hucknall

Sadness

What does it look like?
It looks like you are mad.

What does it feel like?
It feels like you are sad.

What colour is it?
It is the colour blue.

What does it smell like?
It smells like you are sad.

What does it remind you of?
When I was missing my friend who died.

What does it sound like?
It sounds like you are crying.

Amy Smith (7)
Leen Mills Primary School, Hucknall

Surprise

What does surprise smell like?
Surprise smells like a fizzy drink tingling
as you walk through the door.

What does surprise remind you of?
Surprise reminds you of a bowl of delicious ice cream.

What colour is surprise?
Surprise is as purple as a violet.

What does surprise feel like?
Surprise feels like a balloon popped in your head.

What does surprise sound like?
Surprise sounds like fireworks banging.

What does surprise look like?
Surprise looks like a smiling face at a surprise party.

Isabella Sheridan (7)
Leen Mills Primary School, Hucknall

Loneliness

Loneliness is like the blue sky.
Loneliness is like hungriness.
Loneliness makes you want to eat pie.
Loneliness makes you want to cry.
Loneliness makes you want to run.
Loneliness is like the colour black.
Loneliness is like the thunder.
Loneliness makes you get butterflies in your tummy.
Loneliness is what I call bad.
Loneliness is not nice.
Loneliness makes you feel bad.
Loneliness is like the lightning.
Loneliness is like frightened animals.
Loneliness is like a big ball of fire.

Abbie Batey (7)
Leen Mills Primary School, Hucknall

Angry

What colour is it?
Anger is dark red.
What does it taste like?
Anger tastes like burning fire.
What does it feel like?
Anger feels like a bomb exploding inside you.
What does it sound like?
Anger sounds like someone shouting.
What does it look like?
Anger looks like smoke.
What does it remind you of?
Anger reminds me of my mum telling me off.
What does it smell like?
Anger smells like smoke.

Abbie Mountain (8)
Leen Mills Primary School, Hucknall

Calm

Calm looks like the Mediterranean sea
just crossing the beach line.

Calm is the sound of the gentle breeze
whistling through the trees on a summer's day.

Calm moves like the wind gracefully and peacefully
as it whirls through the palm trees.

Calm reminds me of lying on the beach in Hawaii.

Calm smells like a sweet smell
on a calm summer's day.

Calm is pure bliss.

Laura Howe (10)
Leen Mills Primary School, Hucknall

Anger!

Anger is red rage pinning me up against a wall,
Anger is a puff of smoke in my face.

Anger is the fire in my heart burning it up,
Anger is my eyes stinging with pain.

Anger is a prowling tiger ready to pounce,
Anger is red eyes staring in my face.

Anger is tasting the smoke of a fire,
Anger is for us, the taste of milk.

Anger is a screaming kettle,
Anger is the crunch of breaking bones.

Hazel Surgey & Kelsie Symms (10)
Leen Mills Primary School, Hucknall

Feeling Worried

Feeling worried is like feeling
you're going to fall off the top of a mountain.
Feeling worried sounds like footsteps
coming closer and closer.
Feeling worried looks like a tiger
with gleaming red eyes coming closer to you.
Feeling worried feels like a puff of smoke
coming right into your face.
Feeling worried is purple, like a dark sky
on Hallowe'en night.
Feeling worried tastes like cold water in a lake.

Kiera Tarpey (8)
Leen Mills Primary School, Hucknall

Joyful

Joyful is like a baby laughing.
Joyful is like a rainbow shooting across the sky.
Joyful is like an angel flying through the heavens.
Joyful smells like the ocean swaying in the breeze.
Joyful smells like a horse's tail, swishing in the air.
Joyful smells like red roses.
Joyful looks like big flowers.
Joyful feels like the feathers on my feet.
Joyful tastes like strawberries.
Joyful sounds like birds singing in the trees.

Isaac Samuel Payne (8)
Leen Mills Primary School, Hucknall

Happiness

Happiness is when you are walking on the beach.
Happiness is when you are eating your Sunday dinner.
Happiness is when a baby has just been born.
Happiness is like a smooth pear.
Happiness is green, like the green grass swaying.
Happiness is orange, like leaves crunching.
Happiness is like every colour in the rainbow.
Happiness is yellow, like the blazing sun.
Happiness is a lime green apple.
Happiness is like the sun setting every night.

Sam Williams (9)
Leen Mills Primary School, Hucknall

Calm

Calm feels like a soft quilt on a comfy bed.
Calm tastes like a strawberry covered in chocolate.
Calm reminds me of a beautiful butterfly.
Calm looks like snowflakes floating down.

Jodie Elise Mayfield (10)
Leen Mills Primary School, Hucknall

Darkness

Darkness is when you're all alone on the street, cold and hungry.
Darkness is when you're freezing cold and blue.
Darkness sounds like someone's crying for help, all alone.
Darkness is black, like the middle of the night.
Darkness smells like a hot fire.
Darkness looks like a room with no lights on.
Darkness feels like there's no one for you.
Darkness feels like you are in Heaven.
Darkness is when you're all alone in a black room.
Darkness tastes like the soot out of a chimney.

George Steven Harris (8)
Leen Mills Primary School, Hucknall

Feeling Surprised

Feeling surprised is like the sun setting in the evening.
Feeling surprised is like a spider jumping out at you.
Feeling surprised is like someone giving you a present.
Feeling surprised is the sound of birds singing in the trees.
Feeling surprised is the taste of salty fresh air.
Feeling surprised looks like my friends are having fun.
Feeling surprised is red, like having a new friend.
Feeling surprised is blue, like dolphins jumping in and out of the water.

Jessica Parrish (8)
Leen Mills Primary School, Hucknall

Joyful

Joyful is black like a blackberry.
Joyful is like my pet hamster crawling over me.
Joyful smells like a rosy cherry pie.
Joyful is like your TV gleaming at you.
Joyful is like winning the lottery.

Brooklyn Evans (8)
Leen Mills Primary School, Hucknall

Happiness

Happiness is the first day I got my horse.
Happiness is the sweet smell of the beautiful air
where you can be free.
Happiness is where you are really excited for something
you're looking forward to.
Happiness is a room of bright yellow smiley faces.
Happiness is the colour of a red heart.
Happiness is the trotting of a horse winning the horse show
jumping their way to the trophy.

Alex Lauren Hopewell & Nici Landay (10)
Leen Mills Primary School, Hucknall

Love!

Love is the red colour of your beating heart.
Love is the smell of fully grown roses.
Love is the sound of little children waking up on Christmas morning.
Love is the movement of lovebirds kissing.
Love is the reminder of your parents when you're born.
Love is the feeling of your first kiss.
Love looks like the first day of your secondary school life.
Love tastes like chocolate melting in your mouth.

Aiden Pacey (10)
Leen Mills Primary School, Hucknall

Feeling Worried

Feeling worried is like starting school.
Feeling worried is like being scared.
Feeling worried is like going on a plane for the first time.
Feeling worried sounds like thunder in the dark.
Feeling worried tastes like spicy chicken.
Feeling worried looks like a dark, gloomy room.
Feeling worried is dark blue.

Lacey Williamson (7)
Leen Mills Primary School, Hucknall

74

Peace

Peace is the calm sound of the peace hippies of the sixties.
Peace moves like a pride of lions, fierce but proud, basking in the sun.
Peace reminds me of the chugging Volkswagen Beetle.
Peace is as white as a dove's wing.
Peace looks like the colourful bubbles in a lava lamp.
Peace is a soft feather from a dove.
Peace tastes like a crisp drop of pure water.

Zac Jordan (10)
Leen Mills Primary School, Hucknall

Calm

Calm is a light blue sky with floating, colourful bubbles.
Calm is a baby in a deep sleep.
Calm is the taste of a drip of the finest, bluest water.

Calm reminds me of the big splashing waves, crashing back
to the ground, on a lovely paradise golden beach,
with a beautiful blue sky.

Calm is the colour of light pink clouds.

Hollie Evans (9)
Leen Mills Primary School, Hucknall

Darkness

Darkness is like loads of eyes watching you.
Darkness is when you are alone on a street.
Darkness is like millions of black worms.
Darkness is when you walk in the pitch-black.
Darkness is like black killer whales jumping in the water.
Darkness sounds like a ghost haunting you.

Mark Turner (8)
Leen Mills Primary School, Hucknall

Feeling Grateful

Feeling grateful is golden, like a golden butterfly fluttering.
Feeling grateful is blue, like the waves swishing.
Feeling grateful looks like shining rain.
Feeling grateful feels like shaking your friend's hand.
Feeling grateful sounds like someone shouting my name.
Feeling grateful smells like roses blooming in the sun.

Libby Smith (9)
Leen Mills Primary School, Hucknall

Joyful

Joyful is like the wind blowing the bluebells.
Joyful is like the waterfall in the sea.
Joyful is a bit of peace on your own.
Joyful is trees blowing in the wind.
Joyful is like the waves swishing in and out.
Joyful is like you are painting the sea.

Alex Humphreys (8)
Leen Mills Primary School, Hucknall

Happiness

Happiness is the nature in the meadow.
Happiness is like the birds tweeting in the trees.
Happiness is like baby robins in my auntie's garage.
Happiness is like walking in when it is Christmas.
Happiness is like rain dripping in a puddle.
Happiness is like when my sister brings me a present.

Aaron Holmes-Parker (9)
Leen Mills Primary School, Hucknall

Anger

Anger is the feeling of a bright red sun burning to a crisp.
Anger is the smell of toxic gas and burnt sausages.
Anger is the sound of a lion's roar, hunting for its prey.
Anger is the colour of a spicy red pepper.
Anger is the taste of rotten fruit turning to mush in your mouth.
Anger moves like a killer whale searching for its enemy.

Natalie Walpole (10)
Leen Mills Primary School, Hucknall

Calm

Calm is the taste of the fresh mint air blowing freely.
Calm is the smell of a cake being cut into pieces.
Calm moves like an eagle soaring in the sky.
Calm is the sound of a perfect purr from a tabby cat.
Calm is the colour of a brown tomcat resting on a sofa.

Callum James Gillan (10)
Leen Mills Primary School, Hucknall

Feeling Grateful

Feeling grateful is blue, like the swishing waves.
Feeling grateful looks like summer flowers blooming.
Feeling grateful is yellow like the golden sun.
Feeling grateful is like having a new bedroom.
Feeling grateful is like winning a prize at the fair.

Angel Challand (8)
Leen Mills Primary School, Hucknall

Happiness

Happiness is like winning a marathon and coming in first place.
Happiness is bright lime green, as sweet as a juicy apple.
Happiness tastes like an exotic kiwi fruit on a summer's day.
Happiness is like a horse galloping through a field.
Happiness is as circular as a clock ticking throughout the day.

Maje Felten (9)
Leen Mills Primary School, Hucknall

Peace

Peace is the moment a white dove sweeps down off a great oak tree.
Peace is the smell of a strawberry-scented candle burning.
Peace feels like a chocolate, everlasting, bubble bath.
Peace tastes like marshmallows dipped in a chocolate fountain.
Peace is a colourful rainbow in the sunny sky.

Arabel Clark (9)
Leen Mills Primary School, Hucknall

Anger

Anger moves as sly as a fox out hunting on a dark night.
Anger is a deafening scream from an aggressive man.
Anger is the smell of smoke coming from a blazing fire.
Anger has the colour of blood red from an injured warrior.
Anger is like a thousand bees buzzing around you.

Ellie Webster (10)
Leen Mills Primary School, Hucknall

Love

Love is like a thousand roses.
Love is like a dolphin.
Love is like a white swan.
Love is lovely green grass.
Love is like a thousand sea creatures.

Sebastian Grant
Leen Mills Primary School, Hucknall

Feeling Surprised

Feeling surprised is like your friend jumping up and scaring you.
Feeling surprised is like a surprise party.
Feeling surprised is like seeing an angel high in the sky.
Feeling surprised is like getting a medal.
Feeling surprised is like Coca-Cola splashing all over your face.

Georgia Buttress (8)
Leen Mills Primary School, Hucknall

Love

Love is the colour of baby-pink clouds.
Love is the movement of Cupid's arrow flying through the air.
Love is a luscious red heart, beating when you see your love.
Love is your favourite juicy sweet.
Love is the smell of the most expensive perfume.

Katrina Ellingworth (10) & Holly Davis
Leen Mills Primary School, Hucknall

Anger

Anger is a red chameleon hiding on a red leaf.
Anger is a hungry grizzly bear.
Anger is a smelly dog who you are looking for.
Anger is getting slapped round the face.
Anger is the pain of a wasp stinging you.

Olivia Georgia Bell (10)
Leen Mills Primary School, Hucknall

Joyful

Joyful is like being happy on a summer's day.
Joyful is orange like a dandelion.
Joyful is bouncy like a bouncy ball.
Joyful is strong like a piece of metal.
Joyful is excitement slipping through your fingers.

Jack Mountain (8)
Leen Mills Primary School, Hucknall

Feelings Poem!

Calm is like a jellyfish deep in the sea.
Calm smells like a pretty flower in the meadow.
Calm tastes like the sweet crunch of a strawberry.
Calm looks like bubbles floating in the bright blue sky.
Calm feels like a tropical ocean coming to shore.

Georgia Arslan (11) & Chloe Crane (10)
Leen Mills Primary School, Hucknall

Peace

Peace is the moment a white dove swoops down off a great oak tree.
Peace is the smell of a strawberry candle burning.
Peace feels like a chocolate, everlasting bubble bath.
Peace tastes like marshmallows dipped in a chocolate fountain.
Peace is a colourful rainbow in the sunny sky.

Bethany Horobin (9)
Leen Mills Primary School, Hucknall

Happiness

Happiness is the yellow of a euphoric face with a big, bright smile.
Happiness is a giggle of a happy toddler.
Happiness looks like a quiet summer evening on the beach.
Happiness smells like a floral garden in full bloom.
Happiness moves like a child on Christmas morning.

Flynn Asher (9)
Leen Mills Primary School, Hucknall

Fear

Fear is a big hairy spider injecting venom in a fly.
Fear is the colour of black, silently spreading across a room.
Fear is the sound of a screaming ghost floating around a castle.
Fear is the taste of crimson blood leaking from an injured arm.

Jonathon Clinkscale (10)
Leen Mills Primary School, Hucknall

Happiness

Happiness is pink flowers.
Happiness feels like a warm hug from your mum.
Happiness is the smell of a tasty Sunday dinner bubbling in the oven.
Happiness is playing football.

Paul Adams & Joshua Bellamy (10)
Leen Mills Primary School, Hucknall

Music

Music is life,
Music is soul,
Music is everything,
Music is Michael Jackson,
'And who better for music than Michael Jackson?'
Thriller or Bad
Beat It or Billie Jean
Black Or White

So many choices, yet people say,
Music is rap
Music is R&B
Music is Kanye West
And who better for music than KW?'
Heartless to Heartbreak
Paranoid to Gold Digger
Robot Cop to American Boy
But we can all agree
Music is important.

Caleb Peace (10)
Mapperley Plains Primary School, Mapperley

Me And Lily

Me and my best friend Lily
Sometimes do things we shouldn't do,
We trick my sister's friend Milly,
And shove teddies down the loo.

When we get to school we do our secret handshake.
After we have played in the pool,
We have a jug of milkshake.

When my mum finds out she says . . .
'No
More
Pudding
For
You
Two.'

So we find something better to do.

We raid the fridge,
So we eat too much ice cream,
Then we step in a big ditch,
After we make our science project, 'Steam'.

Now guess what my mum says,
'No
More
Pudding
For
You
Two.'

Erin Cartwright (10)
Mapperley Plains Primary School, Mapperley

Me And My Neighbour

Me and my neighbour Jasmine,
we sit in my room,
telling our biggest secrets.

We play on our DSs
and draw pictures.
Then my little sisters come!

They ruin everything!
'I want to sit next to Jas.'
'You can't sit next to Jas, Niamh!'

I go to my mum
and tell her the problem.
She goes, 'Let them sit next to her.'

Then I say, 'That's not fair!'
So my mum moves them,
then I sit next to Jas.

Then we get drinks,
Jas normally has apple juice,
so she gets her apple juice.

Then here come my sisters again!
They go, 'I want apple juice like Jas!'
They are so annoying!

They follow us everywhere!
When we're on the laptop,
they come in my room and say,
'Come on Jas, let's go!'

Jas ignores them and they get bored,
and go! (At last).
About 20 minutes later they're back,
to get them away Jas plays with them for a bit.

When she comes back down,
she sits down and tells me what they did,
and then I say, 'Boring!'

We both laugh,
and enjoy the peaceful time we've got,
before they invade again!

Niamh Orange (10)
Mapperley Plains Primary School, Mapperley

Happy Is A Place

Happy is a place
That is colourful and light.
Like the sun shining bright
Over the world.

Happy is a place that is
Cheerful and bright.
Like the world below my feet.
When it is colourful and bright,
I always go there.

Happy is a place
That's funny and friendly.
That is always nice
And never bites.

Happy is a place
That is fun and bright.
Where you always eat
How much you like.

Greg McLean (9)
Mapperley Plains Primary School, Mapperley

Fighting

By the lake we're fighting again
My little brother has gone insane
Saying the water is lower than him.
I say, 'No, it's not,'
And I step in
Splash!
'Help, help!'

In the shop we're fighting again
My little brother has gone insane
Saying, 'I can push you far away.'
I say, 'No you can't.'
But he does anyway
Crash!
I say, 'I know I like beans but not this much.'

In the lounge we're fighting again
My little brother has gone insane
Saying, 'Batman is better than Spider-Man any day.'
I say, 'No, he's not.'
And he shoves me away
Smash!
'Uh-oh, Mum's new vase!'

'Kate, they're fighting again.'
'What about this time?'
'I think it's a game.'

George Montgomery (9)
Mapperley Plains Primary School, Mapperley

Trouble

Me and my brother
We like to tease my dad,
We love it!
Every time I do something wrong,
He goes,
'Do
Not
Do
That
Again!'
And there's my brother,
Laughing and saying,
'Do
Not
Do
That
Again!'
I can't help laughing,
My dad's not stupid,
He knows something's going on.
We both get into big trouble!

We go to bed without being fed,
We fall asleep
Counting sheep.

The next morning I get into trouble
And there's my brother behind my dad's back saying . . .
You've guessed it!

Curtis Clifford (9)
Mapperley Plains Primary School, Mapperley

My Baby Brother

My baby brother
the son of my mother
he loves to fight
with all his might.

Unfortunately with us
he makes a fuss
sometimes I wish
he was a fish

I'd put him in a bowl
that's my goal
life would be easy
if he was a mole

He cries a lot
when he's told to not
fuss and fight
all day and night

He was sweet
when he was born
wish he was big
so he could mow the lawn

Nevertheless
I love him to bits
When I put him to bed
I give him a kiss.

Anisa Malik (10)
Mapperley Plains Primary School, Mapperley

Me And My Best Friend

Me and my best friend
support each other
and laugh at one another.
He makes me smile
he's also as tall as the River Nile.

He's fast at running
and his plans are always cunning.
He loves his computer
even more than his Ben 10 scooter.

He likes Facebook
and his mum's a good cook.
We dress up like crooks
and then he gets his rubber hooks.

He likes milk
and loves his kilt
he likes playing football
He also likes to play on Paris Hilton's Mall Rall

We play Mellish RFC
and we push
then pant
and sometimes we can't.
We also sweat
and we become very wet.

Nicholas White (10)
Mapperley Plains Primary School, Mapperley

Happy Feelings

I'm happy
When I go on holidays
To Lanzarote or Cornwall
What amazing days

I'm excited
When I'm on roller coasters
At Alton Towers
That's on all the posters

I'm jubilant
When I'm at a friend's house
She has a cute pet
A furry brown mouse

I'm cheerful
When I read a book
Go ice-skating
Swimming or cook.

I'm always happy!

Amber Rose Burbidge (11)
Mapperley Plains Primary School, Mapperley

Me And My Friend Niamh

Me and my friend Niamh
are always at the end of the line for dinner
and she can make funny faces.
At sports day she wins all the races
so it means she is the winner.
We have most great days
but especially on Fridays
when we have a sleepover.
When it's my, or her, birthday
we buy each other presents
and we both say *'Hip hip hooray!'*

Jenna Ly Erasmus (10)
Mapperley Plains Primary School, Mapperley

I Had A Dream

I had a dream that people
Were made of cream,
I dreamt that the world
Was made of curls,
And cars, made of chocolate bars,
Roads were made of toads,
And walls, made of balls,
Drawers had claws,
Doors had jaws,
Doors were friends with drawers,
Cars were made from Mars,
Houses made of mouses,
Plants even danced,
Trees had knees,
What a weird dream I had.

Harvey Priestley (10)
Mapperley Plains Primary School, Mapperley

Me And My Sister

Me and my sister
Laugh at my mum
When she bangs her head
And all she says is,
'Stop laughing.'
So we run upstairs
And we giggle all day
On our beds
We come back down
Still giggling and all we hear is
'Stop laughing.'
So we sit on the sofa
With a smile on our faces
And all we hear is
'Stop laughing!'

Olivia Lee-Brown (9)
Mapperley Plains Primary School, Mapperley

No

'Nathan, it's time to go to bed.'
'No.'
'It's time to go to *bed!*'
'No.'
'I'll get your ted.'
'No.'
'All right, you win.'
Yessss . . .'

'Nathan, it's time to get out of bed.'
'No.'
'It's time to get out of *bed!*'
'No.'
'I heard it's superhero week at school.'
'Oh yeah.'

'It wasn't superhero week.'
'Really, well it's bedtime.'
'No!'

Nathan Holroyd (9)
Mapperley Plains Primary School, Mapperley

The Sleepover

Me and my friends
are in a tent,
all having fun,
all the way to Kent.

We hear a noise,
very scary,
it looks quite fat,
it's a cat that's hairy.

We're all snuggled up
in a soft bed,
Bump,
bump,
bump,
I think
that's someone's head,
I hope there's no lump!

Manisha Johal (10)
Mapperley Plains Primary School, Mapperley

Me And My Mum

Me and my mum
Play together all day
We have a good day

But when he's back
We act normal
The dogs go down
The cats go down
The fish go down
Because Dad's back

And he says, 'I've got a lack
Of sleep. As well as that,
What's
for pudding?
Watch out, watch out Dad's about!

Alexandra Wright (9)
Mapperley Plains Primary School, Mapperley

Juicy Fruity

Watering in my mouth
Like an orange would do.
Queue up for some fruit
We have got a long queue.
Next door to us we have got some stew
And some drinks just for you.
You must eat fruit it is healthy for you.
Juicy fruity here I come
We have got fruit for everyone!
Grapes, bananas and pears too just for 99p
So please be proud just for me.
Bananas are yellow
Oranges are orange
Strawberries are red with slight green dots
And a green stem.

Alicia Anthoney (8)
Northfield Primary & Nursery School, Mansfield Woodhouse

94

Dancing

Dancing, dancing, 1, 2, 3,
Keep your rhythm moving with me.
The sound of the music
Makes us move,
So come on and join in
And get in the groove.
Dancing, dancing it makes us move,
Everything in our bodies swing,
Ripleys and body rolls,
Splits and head rolls,
Points and get up off the walk,
It does it all.
Dancing, dancing, it sure is good
Everybody moving every day.
Do dancing three times a day
And you will be fit.
Dancing, dancing always makes you happy.
Keep your body strong.

Natasha Ingleby (10)
Northfield Primary & Nursery School, Mansfield Woodhouse

Hallowe'en Night

It's a spooky Hallowe'en night
Everywhere's a fright
There's shivering here
And shivering there.
It's a spooky Hallowe'en night
It's a spooky Hallowe'en night
Skeletons are white as ghosts
Witches fly and pumpkins lie
It's a spooky Hallowe'en night
It's a spooky Hallowe'en night
It's a spooky Hallowe'en night
It's a spooky, spooky, scary, scary *Hallowe'en night!*

Bethany Doe (8)
Northfield Primary & Nursery School, Mansfield Woodhouse

This Is The Dragon

He sits majestically with pride,
Guarding all of his precious treasure.
His demon eye catches a glimpse of the sun outside,
This is the dragon I will ride.

With a furnaced breath of raging fire,
His knife-like talons stab the cave roof.
With a struggle he climbs higher,
This is the dragon that is a flyer.

In the autumn sun with the last falling leaf,
He stretches his wings out wide.
Only to reveal glistening scales beneath,
This is the dragon with the razor-sharp teeth.

With a powerful leap he reaches for the sky,
Curious about the world below.
He swoops around to see what he can spy,
This is a dragon with the penetrating eyes.

Jake Allwood (10)
Northfield Primary & Nursery School, Mansfield Woodhouse

Splunge In The Wall

Seeking at the ghostly house
She bellowed to find a flying mouse.
As the girl approached the door
She was distraught to find an apple core.
As she finished her wander around
She got to a room where nothing was found.
Something was odd about the mouldy wallpaper
As it was painted by a caretaker.
She looked at the disturbing wall
As she spotted green drool!

Sarah Richardson (11)
Northfield Primary & Nursery School, Mansfield Woodhouse

Woodhouse Colts

Woodhouse Colts, Woodhouse Colts
Dribbling up the football field.
Kick, kick, kick, kick, kick, kick.

As big as an elephant
As strong as a brick
And as scary as a tiger
It's Woodhouse!

Woodhouse Colts, Woodhouse Colts
Dribbling up the football field.
Kick, kick, kick, kick, kick, kick.

Woodhouse Colts
They can score
From Kieran to Luke
To Callum to Josh
To the back of the net.

Luke Wyng (10)
Northfield Primary & Nursery School, Mansfield Woodhouse

The Dog, Ray

There was once a dog called Ray,
Who liked to run away.
We tied him to the tree,
But he always managed to break free.

We bought him lots of toys,
To try and keep him busy,
But after a while he'd get bored
And start to be rather silly.

We'd have to chase him down the street,
So he did not have us beat,
But after a while he would win
And we would end up giving in.

Lewis Bishop (10)
Northfield Primary & Nursery School, Mansfield Woodhouse

The Object Collector
(Inspired by 'The Sound Collector' by Roger McGough)

A man dressed in blue was carrying a black bag,
He was collecting objects like:

The homework of my brother,
The breakfast of my mum,
The car keys of my dad,
The handbag of my mum.

The engine of a car,
The brick from a home,
The wheel from a car,
The nappy from a baby.

The kids' jumpers,
The teachers' wages,
The school door,
The school dictionaries.

Ross Heslin (8)
Northfield Primary & Nursery School, Mansfield Woodhouse

My Dog

My dog Max
He's like a white sheet
He runs around barking
And nibbles your feet.

He's always up to no good
Digging and rolling in the mud
Which isn't very good for our bath tub.
My dog Max.

Charlie Stacey (10)
Northfield Primary & Nursery School, Mansfield Woodhouse

Bob Wants A Job

There was a man named Bob
Who wanted a job.
He said to his wife, Sue,
'What should I do?'
'You could be a zookeeper
but watch the lions don't eat ya!
You could be a movie star
and drive a fancy car.
You could be a firefighter
teach kids not to play with a lighter!
You could be a midwife
and bring in a new life.
You could be a sportsman
learn to run as fast as you can!'
Bob didn't know what to do
Nor did his wife Sue!

Chloe Cooke (10)
Northfield Primary & Nursery School, Mansfield Woodhouse

Holiday Adventure

This is a poem about my holiday adventure
When I went down south to Lizard Peninsula.
The sun was hot and the sea was cold.
I had a Cornish pasty that the seagulls got hold of.

The next day we went to the beach
The tide came in and swept us off our feet.
My dad went fishing on a small boat
I had a cream tea which is jam and a scone.

Rhianna Bircumshaw (10)
Northfield Primary & Nursery School, Mansfield Woodhouse

The Silly Nonsense Poem

Silly nonsense, silly nonsense,
Swigly bop, swigly bop,
Ning nang nong, ning nang nong,
It's a nonsense poem.

Silly nonsense, silly nonsense,
Bingy bong, bingy bong,
Toterly teeth, toterly teeth,
It's a nonsense poem.

Silly nonsense, silly nonsense,
Piperly pip, piperly pip,
Lipy loo, lipy loo,
It's a nonsense poem.

It's a nonsense poem,
Now it's time to go.

Emily Allden (8)
Northfield Primary & Nursery School, Mansfield Woodhouse

Space

Space is a gloomy world,
Nothing can be heard.

But a quick flash of some stars
Heading for Mars.

The crunch of some aliens eating the moon,
With a great big spoon.

The noise of a fiery rocket
Way bigger than a pocket.

All the planets, even Mars,
Bigger than one million stars.

Stars are bright,
Brighter than a candlelight.

Daniel Shaw (8)
Northfield Primary & Nursery School, Mansfield Woodhouse

Christmas

My first Christmas was very jolly,
And I got pricked by some holly.
There were piles of snow
And people putting up mistletoe.
There were snow fights
And people thought that they had frostbite.
People were so excited, they threw up
And now they're poorly, they don't want to get up!

Joel Mellors (9)
Northfield Primary & Nursery School, Mansfield Woodhouse

Football And Me

My name is Callum and I am eleven.
I play football 24/7.
Inside, outside, my feet are never still.
I like to win the game and when I score it's brill.
My mates all feel the same
About this wonderful game.
We'll play until we drop,
Because we never stop.

Callum Wilkinson (11)
Northfield Primary & Nursery School, Mansfield Woodhouse

My Hero

He saved my life when I jumped into a pool,
He is strong and caring, funny and cool.
He works hard for money to buy the things I like,
He even taught me to ride my bike.
He comes to watch me play football in the sun or rain,
He picks me up and hugs me when I am in pain.
He loves me whether I'm good or bad,
He is my hero, he is my dad!

Lewis Maskery (10)
Northfield Primary & Nursery School, Mansfield Woodhouse

My Cat!

My cat thinks she's a dog,
She even drinks out the bog.
She's ginger and fluffy,
A little bit scruffy,
And chases the garden frogs.

Tori-J Marriott (10)
Northfield Primary & Nursery School, Mansfield Woodhouse

Look For The Buzzards

My buzzard soared magnificently
Over my head with his feathers stretched
He was as graceful as a dancer.

When he flew he made a whistling
Sound, when I called
He came right back
To me with a screech.

My buzzard was clever
And was strong
In flight, his feathers
Were soft and fluffy.

He was handsome as a dancer
And was a bullet when he flew.

But then came the day
When I flew him free,
When I called he flew
Straight past me
For his life in the wild
Had started!

When he went my heart
Was broken in two
When he flew into the blue.

Harry Jee (7)
North Leverton CE Primary School, Retford

The Eagle's Wish

In the glistening sea full of fish
A fish eagle had a wish
He wished to catch the biggest fish
He knew where it was because it always made a splash

Then he saw something
It was a rainbow; no it was the biggest fish
But the biggest fish was on a dish
And next to the dish
A man, as mean as a dragon was fishing

The eagle swooped down to the dish
But the man ate the fish
Now the eagle wished to catch the second biggest fish

The fish eagle wanted a fish
He was still thinking about the dish
Then he found a different meal, chip shop fish
Now, that's his favourite dish.

Ashleigh Tomlinson (8)
North Leverton CE Primary School, Retford

My Dog Simmo

My dog Simmo
My dog likes to run in a field of bluebells in a peaceful forest

My dog Simmo
He is a big fluffy pillow when he is asleep

My dog Simmo
Is as giddy as a fish and he always knocks people over

My dog Simmo
Is as adorable as a caterpillar curling up

My dog Simmo
Is like a speeding cheetah with flapping ears
feeling the wind on his face.

Holly Simpkins (8)
North Leverton CE Primary School, Retford

My Dog Honey

I like my dog Honey,
She is sometimes ferocious
But sometimes not.

My dog Honey
She guards ducks
Sometimes is clumsy, sometimes cross and stupid.

My dog Honey
She howls at the ice cream man
Once she got bitten and now she is careful.

My dog Honey
She is a friend to everyone and she is a monkey
She is a cute dog!

Yazmin Schofield (8)
North Leverton CE Primary School, Retford

My Animal Poem

I love to watch the fast horses run around,
I like the way they quickly gallop,
Their coats are as white as snow.

I love to watch the feathery eagles fly,
I can hear them squawking in the blue sky,
Their talons are as sharp as tigers' claws.

I love to listen to the fierce tigers roar,
I can see them stalking their prey,
The tigers are like stripy zebras.

I love to watch the scaly snakes slither around,
They slither slowly on the soft ground,
The snakes are scaly dragons.

Amelia Hiner (8)
North Leverton CE Primary School, Retford

The Jungle

If I went in the jungle I would love to see amazing fruit
If I went in the jungle, the flowers would look like a shining rainbow
If I went in the jungle, the grass would feel like a fluffy carpet
If I went in the jungle I would want to hear birds whistling
If I went in the jungle I would like to see tigers roaring
If I went in the jungle I would like to smell amazing flowers
If I went in the jungle I would love to see woodpeckers
cracking a tree
If I went in the jungle I would love to see lots of amazing animals
If I went in the jungle I would love to see tigers looking up
at a rainbow.

Amber Campbell (7)
North Leverton CE Primary School, Retford

In The Field

I can hear baby birds in the nest cheeping for food.

I can smell lovely, vibrant flowers, lots and lots.
The flowers are pretty princesses.

I can taste the delicious fruit, blueberries and blackberries.

I can feel the rabbit's fur, then she shows me her babies.
Their fur is as soft as a teddy bear.

I can see my house in the distance.
I am so lucky to be next to nature.

Grace Archibald (8)
North Leverton CE Primary School, Retford

In Space

I like going to space to land on the moon to see the stars
I like feeling the rough craters as sharp as scissors
I like the moon as bright as starlight
I like seeing the sparkly bright stars
I like seeing shooting stars zooming past the moon
I like going to collect the mess that the aliens left behind
I like going to see the small green aliens.

I quickly left space in my rocket
Because the aliens were scary as dinosaurs.

Katy Reed (7)
North Leverton CE Primary School, Retford

Australia

Koalas eat happily in the trees,
Whilst wallabies hop up and down under,
Kangaroos jump with their babies
As the kookaburra laughs with his lover.

Crocs show a sly smile,
Whilst whale sharks swim
Fairy penguins pile
As soon as the Tasmanian devil has a trim.

The lizards forage
As the lyre bird sings his beautiful song.
The babbling billabong ripples in the shining sun
Whilst frogs croak on lush green lily pads.

The Aborigines play didgeridoos
In the mid-evening mist
Whilst the sun goes down
And the cool damp night draws in.

Alexandra West (9)
Oxley Primary School, Shepshed

106

The Night

One quiet and peaceful evening,
All you could hear was people breathing.
'Get to bed at once!' my mum declares,
So I drag myself up the stairs.

I wait until about 9 o'clock,
I watch the second hand as it goes tick-tock.
The world changes into a different place,
With spooky eyes watching my face.

Soon there is a slight breeze,
With the wind whistling through the trees.
Shadows creep out of their hiding places,
With the sense of danger on their faces.

All of the clouds have come out too,
With their angry glances fixed on you!
It looks like it's going to thunder and lightning,
Tonight is extremely frightening!

The clouds threaten the lightning to do as they say,
The lightning stares at them in dismay.
An unseen flash takes a trip to the ground,
Creating commotion and deafening sound.

When all of this had gone away,
The sky looked strangely like day!
According to my clock it was morning already!
I was still lying there clutching my teddy.

Eleanor Furber (8)
Oxley Primary School, Shepshed

Autumn

Crunch, golden, brown, crispy,
Clump, chop, red, slow, fast,
Rusty colours running.

Lois Poxon (9)
Oxley Primary School, Shepshed

The Day

Come on it's dinner time.
Jack turn off your Xbox you've been playing on it all day long.
Georgia stop winding Jack up.
Come on it's dinner time!

Georgia stop moaning about your vegetables and eat them.
Lauren don't give Jack all your food.
Jack now you're finished go and cover up the rabbit.
Georgia stop moaning about your vegetables and eat them!

Go to bed now Georgia and Lauren!
Jack you can stay down for a little longer
But first go and take the ironing up.
Georgia and Lauren go to bed!

Everyone wake up!
Georgia wake up right now!
Jack stop sleeping sleepyhead.
Everyone wake up!

It's time for school, right,
Georgia make you and Lauren some cereal.
Jack get some toast, it's time for school.
Argh! Peace at last!

Georgia Newbold (10)
Oxley Primary School, Shepshed

Water

Water is such a wonderful thing,
You can get so many types of water.
Rainwater, flavoured water, spring water,
Clean water, dirty water.
You wouldn't live without water,
So just think when you're saying, 'Water, horrible and boring.'
Because actually it's not.

Chelsea Doris (10)
Oxley Primary School, Shepshed

Under The Sea

Under the sea where fish swim free and starfish lie on the rocks,
Dolphins dip and dive, slip and slide gliding through the water,
Diving out and in, swimming within the deep blue depths of the sea.
Octopus so slimy, filled with pitch-black ink,
So you don't want to scare them because you'll be covered
with ink.
Jellyfish will sting you if you get too close,
Crabs are very pinchy, be careful, don't get too near,
Whales shoot water out of their blow holes,
Sharks will nibble on your knees,
Eels are so snake-like they'll give you an electric shock.
They sneak around in the coral and hide in caves of the sea.
Life under the sea is amazing, it looks so much fun,
I wish I was a fish, I'd swim around all day,
I'd play with my friends and have lots of fun and swim till the
day is done.

James King (9)
Oxley Primary School, Shepshed

We Are All Friends

We are all friends, yes we are
So come on everybody cram in my car.
If you get hurt we'll help you
And then a clever doctor will help you too.
As you see we're very kind
Especially if you're poorly or blind.
I've got cookies, do you want some?
These will definitely fill your tum.
I like you, do you like me?
If I come close will I see?
You're very kind, yes you are
If you like you can play on my guitar.
You're the best and you're cool
Now come on, let's sit on a stool.

Lucy Williams (9)
Oxley Primary School, Shepshed

Shut Up

'I'm going out to play.'
'Why?'
'Because I am.'
'Why?'
'I am going to my friend's for tea.'
'Why?'
'Because I am.'
'Why?'
'To get away from you.'
'Why?'
'Because you are annoying.'
'Why?'
'Because you keep saying why.'
'Why?'
'I'm going to my friend's now!'

Hollie Cooper (9)
Oxley Primary School, Shepshed

Get Ready To Go Swimming

Come on children line up please the bus is waiting.
Imogen stop looking at the stick insects!
Come on children, line up please
Amber stop fiddling with your pencil case!
Has everyone got their swimming kit?
At this rate we won't be going.
Amber stop fiddling with your pencil case!
James stop happy bobbing on your chair!
If you haven't got your slip for goggles you can't wear them.
James stop happy bobbing on your chair!
We're ten minutes late.
Zak line up straight!
Stop poking Georgia in the back!
We're ten minutes late.
No swimming now Class 7.

Billie Freeman (9)
Oxley Primary School, Shepshed

Peace At The House

'Dinner time Georgia.'
'Coming Mum, just finishing my homework.'
'Hurry up or your tea will be cold!
Dinner time Georgia.

Georgia you've nearly eaten your tea
would you like some more?'
'No thank you Mum.'
'Georgia you've nearly eaten your tea.

Right bedtime now Georgia.'
'Right, just switching my TV off.'
'Get into bed now Georgia.
Right bedtime now Georgia!'

Georgia Pike (9)
Oxley Primary School, Shepshed

My Rabbit's Dreams

I n the cage my rabbit sits
N ibbling on his carrots
D aydreaming of the great outdoors
I deas of his next great adventures
A s his name is Indian Jones!
N otorious for his climbing skills

J umping up and down, desperate to be free
O ne day he will succeed
N ail-clipping is his second worst fear
E scaping is his plan
S noozing the day away.

Katie West (8)
Oxley Primary School, Shepshed

Little Munchkins

Big ones, small ones, tiny ones, smelly ones,
Clean ones, dirty ones, fat ones, fit ones,
Thin ones, cheeky ones, good ones, bad ones,
Scary ones, hungry ones, fast ones, slow ones,
Mean ones, nice ones, pretty ones, ugly ones,
Funny ones, boring ones, clever ones, sad ones,
Happy ones, curly ones, bold ones, cold ones,
Warm ones, thick ones, red ones, yellow ones,
Purple ones, weird ones, old ones, young ones,
Rough ones, smooth ones, cute ones.
All different munchkins working together.

Jessica Pyle (8)
Oxley Primary School, Shepshed

Two Grannies Discuss Beauty

'How does your hair stay so cobwebby
while mine stays quite white?'
'How did you get that mole on your ugly back?'
'How do you get such hairy legs that look just like they're men's?'
'Why are your ears so big, whilst mine stay quite small?'
'Your neck is just so spotty, look at all those veins.'
'How come you're so podgy?
Do you eat cakes every day?'
'My dear it's nature's beauty, you will never look like me
I am just so beautiful, look at my pale skin.'

Elinor Waite (9)
Oxley Primary School, Shepshed

Poems Are . . .

Poems are lovely.
Poems are the best of all.
Poems are so great.
Poems are better than cake.
Poems are such fun to write.

Holly Taylor (8)
Oxley Primary School, Shepshed

Friends Forever Always Together

Teachers talking,
Friends giggling,
Stomping feet,
Sprinting children
Feet stamping
All together.

Bouncing and pouncing
Sprinting and running,
Balancing and dodging
Walking and diving,
All together.

Faces! Faces! Faces!
Mr MacMaster monster munching,
Gabriella smiling,
Chris crunching,
Me nibbling.

Friends! Friends! Friends!
Neave nattering,
Playing with me,
Sharing with me,
Enjoying playing with me.

Charlotte Hutchings (8)
Ranby CE Primary School, Ranby

Playground Poem

Teachers talking,
Shamus shouting,
Gabriella giggling,
Chattering together.

Sprinting Shamus,
Peter prancing,
Darting past people,
All together.

Faces excited, joyful,
Shamus smiling,
India imagining,
Alby laughing.

Friends trustworthy,
Telling funny jokes,
Helping me when I fall over,
Playing with me.

Friends - funny, happy,
Keep me safe,
As well as playing with me,
Friends smiling together.

Peter Voase (8)
Ranby CE Primary School, Ranby

Friends

Hope running past me
Shamus and Peter playing with me
Tig with TJ, I'm not on.

Teachers chatting
Alby chuckling
Kyle talking.

Cameron Day (8)
Ranby CE Primary School, Ranby

Untitled

Teachers talking,
Chattering together,
Screaming children,
Chattering together.

Skipping and scattering,
Gabriella nattering,
Camille cackling,
Giggling together.

Gabriella grunting,
India imagining,
Molly moaning,
Lexie laughing
All together.

My friends are kind to me,
Isabella plays with me,
We are best friends,
My friends are funny and kind,
Playful all the time,
Sometimes we fall out,
But soon make friends again.

Mia Basilisco (7)
Ranby CE Primary School, Ranby

Friends Forever

Teachers talking
Chatting forever
Like me!

Sprinting, running,
Dodging too
Happy faces
Just like you and me!

Faces chatty, smiley,
Tomas talking
Alby acting
Mia munching
Kane cackling
In the playground.

Me, Peter, Tomas
Talking, chatting,
Alby acting
All together
In the playground.

Shamus Wilson (9)
Ranby CE Primary School, Ranby

Friendship Poem

Teachers chatting, children talking,
Children screaming, children stomping,
People skipping, people clomping,
In the playground people.

Dodging and running and posing,
Dodging and sprinting,
Balancing and darting,
Playing and running.

Faces cheerful, happy, surprised
Mr MacMaster chomping on his banana
Peter was peering through the camera.

Friends keep me safe, cheerful,
Happy, shouting, laughing, talking,
Shocking, surprised
In our playground all together.

Harry Hutchings (8)
Ranby CE Primary School, Ranby

Teachers Talking

Together singing
Children screaming
Gabriella embarrassed.

I can see,
Gabriella running
With her friends
Grace and Ella laughing
People dodging and darting.

Faces -
Excited, cheerful,
Children jumping
Mr MacMaster
Munching on a mango!

Isabella Atkinson (7)
Ranby CE Primary School, Ranby

Best Friends

Teachers chattering,
Children screaming,
Cameron laughing,
Children screaming together!
Jumping and hopping,
Running and skipping,
Giggling together.

Faces - joyful, happy,
Laughing Jack over the moon all together
At the adventure playground.

Friends carefully playing
Joyful, helpful,
Friends together on the playground.

Rhys Garton (8)
Ranby CE Primary School, Ranby

My Sister Does The Funniest Things

My mum and dad told me on Valentine's Day
We had a baby on the way.
We went for a scan yeah, I'm having a sister,
I'm so excited, I can't wait to meet her!

Mum was pregnant forever and ever
Come on baby sister I want us to be together.
One night she was born with a cute little face
I love being a sister, it really is ace!

Now she is bigger she is so much fun
And my mum said she needs eyes in the back of her bum.
She makes funny noises and eats lots of flumps
Her poos are stinky and so are her trumps!

When Mum changes her nappy she loves to wiggle,
So I blow raspberries on her tummy and that makes her giggle.
I love my baby sister we share a bath,
I blow bubbles and we always laugh.

We watch the telly, she loves Iggle Piggle,
When he comes on the screen he makes her giggle.
She needs to learn not to touch
I don't mind 'cause I love her so much!

Eleanor Peacock (8)
Ravenshead CE Primary School, Ravenshead

I Want A Pet Of My Own

I want a pet of my own.
I'd give it a home and buy it a phone.
I want a pet that's funny
A bit like a bunny.
I want a cat
Who knows where it's at.
I want a fox
Who knows how to box
And last of all a dog
Who eats a hog.
I've got enough money to buy a cat
But sometimes they eat rats.
I've got enough money to buy a fox
But I just don't want it to box.
And I've got enough money to buy a dog
But what would I do if it ate a hog?
If I had a pet
It would probably end up at the vets.
Maybe I could imagine I had one
I'd prefer that than having to buy one.

Natalie Purewal (7)
Ravenshead CE Primary School, Ravenshead

Autumn Time Is Here

Leaves falling, birds are calling,
It's autumn time right now!
Change your clocks and pull on your woolly socks
We're covered in leaves . . . *Wow!*
Here comes in sight a wonderful flock of birds in flight
They're gliding through the air, south for the winter.
Whoosh, whoosh the wind is blowing
And everybody keeps on growing.
Chestnuts falling off a tree,
Let's go and collect them, you and me.
Blue sky, what a delight,
Turning dark every night.
Making toffee that's a treat,
Off we go and then we eat.
Guy Fawkes sits upon the fire,
Fireworks shooting higher and higher!

Mollie Garratt (9)
Ravenshead CE Primary School, Ravenshead

My Parents

They are caring,
They are sharing.
They teach you how to put on your clothes,
They teach you how to blow your nose.
They have a hanky when you sneeze,
They teach you manners, mainly please.
They spoil me with all their hard earned money,
I think that is rather funny!
They make my lunch, they make me tea,
They always leave plenty for me.
They never like to leave you alone,
Providing you with a happy home.
They do their very, very best,
But all in all . . . mine beat the rest.

Katie Fuller (9)
Ravenshead CE Primary School, Ravenshead

Mums And Dads

Mums and dads are the best
Be careful they don't rest.
Make sure they care and feed you
Also love and treat you.

Remember to be kind and nice
'Cause sometimes we're like rotten mice.
We're given hugs every day
We should remember to always say,
I love you more than the moon and stars
Because you're definitely the best by far.

Lisha Mae Rayner (9)
Ravenshead CE Primary School, Ravenshead

An Autumn Leaf

A poor leaf lying as still as a statue.
All alone, looking at the dark sky
Time to say, 'Bye.'
When the morning comes children stomp
their feet on the leaf, thinking they are stronger.
Through the day the leaf will sit and think
I want to go home.
No one cares for the poor thing, even the magical tree.
Thinking of a nice warm home and being green like before.
The leaf cannot move and not speak,
A poor leaf alone.

Caitlin Dennison (8)
Redmile CE Primary School, Nottingham

Tunnel Of Kings

Travelling down the eerie tunnel,
danger around every turn,
except there's enough light
to find Pennywise
who is baring the shiny yellow teeth
that are used for killing.
The surrounding darkness,
filled with the scent of murder,
is slowly closing in on you
and the air is escaping.
You are so frightened.
You don't realise Annie Wilkes,
armed with hammer and screaming with anger,
is standing over you.
Suddenly, a burst of golden leaves cave in
and Letand Gaunt charges through the tunnel,
carrying a large bag of unwanted merchandise
from his magic but evil shop.
Quickly, you run away and eventually find the exit.
However, gravestones decorated with masks
are standing around you,
which is strangely intimidating.
You then hear the sound of low growls
and loud hissing.
At the same time,
dark shapes prowl in the moonlit garden.
Horrified you look around
and a cat with glowing red eyes,
weirdly snarls, jumps and attacks.
You know no more.

Kane James Taylor (10)
Redmile CE Primary School, Nottingham

The Robin

The robin flaps suddenly from her nest in the tree.
For the time has come for her to fly, over the treetops
and into the sky.
Calling, cheeping, sometimes sleeping, always flying, never lying.
Getting dark, she sees a little spark, time to sleep.
Morning is coming, bees are humming, chicks are cheeping,
sheep are bleating.
Robin is waking, safe and sound, looks here and there
and then around.
Hops down the tree to let you see . . .
That winter is coming.

Katie Trigg (8)
Redmile CE Primary School, Nottingham

Falling Leaves

What a poor leaf lying on the cold floor
Watching the other gold leaves fall from the tree.
Alone in the dark, watching the moonlight.
Soon it would be day
When the children would come out to play
And poor leaf would say, 'Help! Help!
Oh no, it's day, the children are coming out to play.'
Crunch, crunch goes the poor leaf
None of the leaves could succeed.

Zoe Onyett (8)
Redmile CE Primary School, Nottingham

The Autumn Sky

The autumn sky bigger than an eye
Blows the elegant smooth leaf off a beautiful tree
Slowly drifting down the gold leaves hit the dark damp soil
Like a heavy rock.

Patrick James Hainey (10)
Redmile CE Primary School, Nottingham

The Tree And The Leaf

The rough tree stood high in the sky
Watching his leaves drop like flies.
The leaf at the top not letting go
Watching the flow of his leaves blow.
At last that wind came again
And blew him down just like the rest.
At the bottom he was regretting letting go,
He wished he'd never let go.
Wishing he was the top of the tree.

Josh Brown (9)
Redmile CE Primary School, Nottingham

The Crazy Kite

Swooping, gliding, flying,
Loop the looping, zigzagging,
Whizzing through the sky,
Dancing round in the sky,
The wind drops, so do I.
Sometimes the autumn wind can be so cruel.
Plummeting to the ground
I am falling.
Suddenly the sky feels a million miles away.

Eloise Evans (9)
Redmile CE Primary School, Nottingham

My Leaf Poem

As the leaves fall from the trees
It is a sign that summer has passed.
Gold, brown and yellow the leaves fall
One by one in the autumn breeze.
The leaves are crumpled by the children
As the wind whooshes through the tree.

Chloe Jackson (10)
Redmile CE Primary School, Nottingham

The Autumn Lonely Leaf

One day there was a lonely, cold, crunch leaf,
lying on the rough, hard ground dying for help.
The rustling loud noise made the wind blow
and then suddenly another old crunchy leaf
flew down beside him.
But the leaf that flew down beside him,
it was a nice, smooth, green leaf.
The poor little leaf felt that he had fallen down from the sky
But it had only fallen from a little tree.

Alfie Morley (8)
Redmile CE Primary School, Nottingham

The Lonely Leaf

The leaves sway gently through the breeze.
One leaf that way and the other this;
But one leaf sits on the ground as still as a statue.
The wind blows harder, his face droops.
He just can't.
'What's the matter with me?
All the other leaves can fly, it's just me.
Please help I am struggling.
Please help.'

Hattie Adams (8)
Redmile CE Primary School, Nottingham

Crispy Leaves

Gently the brown, crispy leaves are falling off the trees.
Gently people are walking alone on rough, spiky leaves,
Whilst smelling the pong.
Gently the leaf loses its grip and slowly goes into a dip.
Gently trees get barer but they are aware
Gently the leaves get old like people get cold.

Faye Laywood (10)
Redmile CE Primary School, Nottingham

The Sombre Leaf

Falling softly in the breeze, swooping, looping, gliding, falling.
Landing gently on the covered floor
The little leaf wishing to live for evermore
Guiltily letting go of the branch
Living was his only chance
Lying on the muddy damp floor
Wishing he had more, more, more.

Charlotte Amy Wainwright (10)
Redmile CE Primary School, Nottingham

My Leaf Poem

A brown, red and green leaf sat on the floor.
He wasn't green and beautiful anymore.
Now he was just a boring brown, red and green leaf
Sat on the floor.
His friends were up and happy on the tree.
Oh I wish that could be me.

Lewis Fitzgibbons (8)
Redmile CE Primary School, Nottingham

Autumn

In autumn time so clear and bright
The sun brings love and daylight.
I like autumn because I like all the leaves
crunching on the smooth grassy ground.
The leaves fall off the trees
swaying side to side, swooping in the sky.

Harriet Joyce (8)
Redmile CE Primary School, Nottingham

The Crispy, Golden Leaf

The crispy, golden leaf glided gracefully to the ground.
Sadly, the leaf hoped to be found.
The leaf was gold, brown and crunchy.
Everyone trod on the leaf and he did not feel comfy.
Looking up above at the bright blue sky
The leaf let out a cry, 'Bye-bye.'

Riona Hughes (10)
Redmile CE Primary School, Nottingham

My Poor Little Robin

Poor little robin sitting in the snow
All on its own in the frosty snow.
All the other birds flying in the sky so beautiful,
Shining in the sky, seeing people nice and warm.
People seeing the robin all very cold
Seeing other birds in their homes with other birds.

April Dagpall (8)
Redmile CE Primary School, Nottingham

Forest Football Club

When me and my dad go to football
It's to see my favourite club Forest!
The chanting is loud,
The fans are excited.
When the striker scores a goal
The City Ground explodes.
At half-time I eat a tasty burger
And shake hands with Robin Hood.
The game is almost over
It is time that we went home.
I love going to see Forest,
Just me and my dad.

Thomas David Benton (7)
St John's CE Primary School, Stapleford

A Poem For My Grandma

When I was a baby
She would change my nappy
She calls me her princess
And it makes me happy.

She sends me parcels
A box full of treats
Like games and clothes
And jewellery and sweets.

I sometimes call her
Just to hear her say,
'I love you so much Princess
And I miss you every day.'

She lives so far away
In America you see
But I'll always love my grandma
As much as she loves me.

Josephine Scott (7)
St John's CE Primary School, Stapleford

Who Am I?

I am messy,
I am mucky,
I stay out in the rain,
I washes me.
I like to be stroked
When I play
I push Oliver over
And chase after the ball.

Who am I?

Oliver Townend (7)
St John's CE Primary School, Stapleford

Archie And Me

Outside the school gates it was a nice sunny day.
Nothing could prepare me for what Mum was about to say.
'Archie's moving to Spain,' she said.
I suddenly felt such dread!
How could this be happening to me?
He's my best friend you see.
My heart was beating as fast as a rocket
I wished I could keep Archie in my pocket.

Now that Archie's moved away
I dream about him every day!
I'd like him to be here to dress up as cowboys
To play goodies and baddies and show him my new toys.
We'd run around and shoot each other with toy guns
Make loud noises to annoy our mums!

Bradley Robert Guilford (8)
St John's CE Primary School, Stapleford

A Flying Carpet

We are taking a ride on a flying carpet
High in the sky
Above the trees, the birds and the bees
Clouds floating by,
It's quiet in the sky
Because no one's around
They're all on the ground
We are taking a ride on a flying carpet
High in the sky.

Lauren Wilkinson (8)
St John's CE Primary School, Stapleford

Homework

H is for home and happy
O is for outside and openness
M is for Mum and merry
E is for early and Easter
W is for work and worry
O is for orange and Opal
R is for ready and reading
K is for keeping and kitten
        Homework keeps me busy.

Sophie Marie Sykes (8)
St John's CE Primary School, Stapleford

The Colours Of Flowers

Roses are red,
Violets are blue,
Pansies are purple
And you can smell them too.

Daffodils are yellow,
Tulips are red,
Bluebells are blue
And they smell very, very nice too.

Indya Ann Mason (7)
St John's CE Primary School, Stapleford

Flying Carpet

Flying carpet so light
Swirling, twirling in the blue sky
Looking and seeing you in flight
I wish I could fly with you tonight
When the carpet comes to land
Jump on board to other lands.

Chloe Biggs (8)
St John's CE Primary School, Stapleford

Seasons

Winter
December, January, February, *brr!*
Spring
March, April, May, the lovely breeze.
Summer
June, July, August, hot! hot! hot!
Autumn
September, October, November, trees, leaves.

Lewis Daniel Philip Fisher (8)
St John's CE Primary School, Stapleford

Autumn

It is autumn
As I get out of bed
I look out of the window
All flowers are dead.
Soon Jack Frost will be here
I'd better find my hat and scarf
So I can go to the fair.

Jorge Jackson (7)
St John's CE Primary School, Stapleford

Dreams

I have a dream
To become the greatest footballer on Earth.
I have a dream
To become the best chef on the Earth.
I have a dream
To discover when the glorious Romans began.

Ayomide Adeiga (8)
St John's CE Primary School, Stapleford

Brave Knights

Brave knights wear armour,
Brave knights ride brave horses,
Brave knights fight dragons and other armies
And some can die.

Georgia Lucy Bailey-Clark (8)
St John's CE Primary School, Stapleford

The Loo

Wake up, for goodness sake it's 2.52
Something inside says 'I need the loo'
But I'm far too cosy to switch on the light
I'll just turn my head round and hope it's alright.

Wake up, now it's 3.23
Something calls out 'A wee, wee, wee'
But outside the bed it's really cold
So breath in deep and, ah, I hold.

Wake up, it's 4.28
Something grunts, 'I just can't wait'
But I'm not bothered to get up and walk
So tell that bladder to shut it no more.

Wake up it's 6.00
Something yells 'It's time, I need to get up'
But the sun just reaches the coloured sky
To I tell myself I need not bother, why?

Wake up it's 6.59
Something screams 'It's toilet time!'
So I finally do what I knew I could
And it feels good, oh yes, it feels really good!

Melissa Bonner (10)
St Mary's RC Primary School, Loughborough

Sofa Boat

Sofa boat, sofa boat
   Sailing to sea
      Take me to an island.

Sofa boat, sofa boat
   Sailing to sea
      Take me to a beach.

Sofa boat, sofa boat
   Sailing to sea
      Take me to the sand.

Sofa boat, sofa boat
   Sailing to sea
      Take me to the palm trees.

Sofa boat, sofa boat
   Sailing to sea
      Take me to an island.

Ellena Crowe (8)
St Mary's RC Primary School, Loughborough

Guess Who?

Hand tickler
Furry body
Long sleeper
Drink water
Loves exercise
Large teeth
Big nibbler
Small legs
Fast runner.

What am I?
I am a guinea pig.

George Suffolk & Harvey Clarke (8)
St Mary's RC Primary School, Loughborough

The Gory Story Of Red Riding Hood

Red Riding Hood was going to her gran's one day
When a wolf came walking down her lane.
It spied her like a hawk it did
And then in the shadows he hid.
It pursued her to the house
Quiet as a mouse.
When they finally reached the door
The wolf lay soundless, flat on the floor.
Silently he edged inside
And went under the bed to hide.
As Gran was handed fatty food
She was in a very good mood.
When she'd guzzled all her treats,
She was lovely and sweet, good to eat.
But did she like her treats, yes or no?
Squish, crunch, alas, we'll never know.

Joshua Harry Pimm (11)
St Mary's RC Primary School, Loughborough

Coconut Tree

Coconut tree, coconut tree
In the sea,
Coconut tree, coconut tree
Live with me,
Coconut tree, coconut tree
Giggle with me,
Coconut tree, coconut tree
Funny like me,
Coconut tree, coconut tree
You and me.

Euan Keeler (8)
St Mary's RC Primary School, Loughborough

Rocket

A rocket flies as fast as a cheetah to space
Moved by an engine
When they get to the moon
They see their own rocket on the moon.

When the rocket takes off fire comes out of the engines
Like a bomb or a volcano erupting
Off into space we go
We're going to the planet Jupiter
Off we go, three, two, one - *blast off!*

When they get to the moon there is no moon
It has exploded into space
'Oh no! We will have to go home!'
when they get back to Earth
they go home in their gold car.

Max Crabb (7)
St Mary's RC Primary School, Loughborough

Kathleen Pullan

K ind sometimes
A bit mean
T icklish not!
H ates Teletubbies
L auren is her best friend
E nergetic most of the time
E asy to annoy
N aughty at home.

P icks on me
U ntidy
L oves Dad
L oves Mum
A nnoying
N ormally bossy.

Charlotte Pullan (7)
St Mary's RC Primary School, Loughborough

Michael Jackson

M y best singer
 I s the king in the grave
C an sing the best songs in the world
H as died
A dead singer
E ntertainment
L ively singer

J olly man
A famous pop star
C ame to Los Angeles
K ing of pop
S imilar to a lot of singers
O bliging nice man
N early his birthday.

Sameei Muhammed (7)
St Mary's RC Primary School, Loughborough

The Football Boy

There was a boy who liked football
He went to football
And kept the ball
He wants to play
But needs to pay
He has good tricks
And likes chicks
He is the best
But a bit of a pest.

Toby Snell (8)
St Mary's RC Primary School, Loughborough

What Am I?

Sometimes I am big
I am very round
If you scratch me sometimes I go red
You can see that sometimes people pick me
But I don't like it as it hurts me
I really don't like it
Sometimes I go a different colour . . .

What am I?

Georgia Taylor (8)
St Mary's RC Primary School, Loughborough

JLS

JLS has four people.
Louis was the judge who guided them through the show.
Songs they sang are 'Last Christmas', 'Beat Again'
And lots of other songs.
My favourite one is the short one.
He does most of the singing
And he is good at it.
JLS is a boy group.

Kasia Brown (7)
St Mary's RC Primary School, Loughborough

Light Lodger

Bright shiner
Night burner
Sound creeper
Energy waster
Bright dazzler
White logger

What am I?

Matthew Stretton (8)
St Mary's RC Primary School, Loughborough

Sweeties

S o sticky they stick to your hand.
W hen I have them I want more.
E verybody loves them.
E verywhere they have sugar on them.
T aste yummy like chocolate.
I n packets.
E ver so lovely.
S ticky so much.

Ellie Denton (7)
St Mary's RC Primary School, Loughborough

The World

The world has different colours and
It has different shapes and sizes.
In space there's black sky
But on Earth there's blue sky in the air.
Space has got no air so nobody can breathe.
On Earth there are no dimensions
But in space there are lots of dimensions.

Jan Brix-Amoroso (7)
St Mary's RC Primary School, Loughborough

The Little Cockroach

The little cockroach
Big and small
Not tall
Oh what a relief
It is Dad who is big
Mum who is medium
I'm not big at all!

Ryan Phillips (8)
St Mary's RC Primary School, Loughborough

Dolphin Acrostic Poem

D olphins can sleep with one eye open.
O ver it jumps through the hoop in the water.
L ots of dolphins like to see people.
P eople like to feed dolphins.
H ave a great time with people.
I n the water they like to swim.
N ever harm people!

Sarina Mallick (8)
St Mary's RC Primary School, Loughborough

TV

TV programmes on all the time.
TV, you press numbers to see a programme.
TV is fun.
On TV you can change channels.
On TV you can watch programmes.
TV feels hard.

Henry Jackson (7)
St Mary's RC Primary School, Loughborough

Lightning Bolt

One big lightning struck and it went straight through a fat duck.
One big lightning struck and a chicken went cluck, cluck, cluck.
One big lightning struck and a man took a look.
One big lightning struck and a lady went *zookuck!*
One big lightning struck and the town shook.
One enormous lightning struck and the world blew up in one *strike*.

Ciaran Moreland (8)
St Mary's RC Primary School, Loughborough

The Body

Pump, pump, pump!
If you did not have a heart
Where would your blood go?

If you did not have a heart
Where would your lungs go?

William Pimm (8)
St Mary's RC Primary School, Loughborough

The World

The world has lots of different colours on our planet.
It is lots bigger than a house.
There are millions of countries.
There are lots of languages.
Lots of oceans that are very big.

Samuel Flanagan (7)
St Mary's RC Primary School, Loughborough

Games

G ames are good
A lready lots of games are out
M any people like games
E verybody thinks games are good
S ome are better than good!

Mekha Thomas (8)
St Mary's RC Primary School, Loughborough

Kiss Me Not

Roses are red
Violets are blue
Please don't kiss me
Because I have the flu!

Nkem Eleode (8)
St Mary's RC Primary School, Loughborough

The Genie Without A Lamp

Once this genie named Adil was sick and ill.
For all he could do was cry and shout, 'Boo-hoo!'
He went to his lamp.
When his mistress came in and said,
'Go to bed Adil, this is no time for a game!'
She rubbed the lamp but nothing came out
except for a small genie's head who came to say,
'Look at Adil, he is ill and sick,
for I will be your genie right down from a click!
For every wish and every command,
I will grant it, from the top of my hand.
Oh Mistress what will you plead?'
'I wish Adil was better
and that you were not my genie anymore.'
'No!'
Suddenly, out of sight, the genie police came out from the night.
'You must grant that wish,' they said, 'or you will have to pay
the price.'
'Though I also wish you didn't exist and you'd just disappear right
into the mist.'
'Oh well, here I go, with a click of my hand you will know!'
Now he's gone Adil is back
And he feels better than ever and not bad!

Thomas Clayton (9)
Thringstone Primary School, Coalville

Bubblegum

Chewy, chewy bubblegum.
All the different flavours are so yum, yum.
I love bubblegum.
I dream of bubblegum,
Big or small,
Sticky or sweet.
In my dreams I fall fast asleep.
The colours are pink, green, black or blue.
When my jaw aches
I know I'm through.
Bubbly, bubbly, bubbly gum.
When I blow the biggest bubble
I know that I am done!

Emily Grace Usher (10)
Thringstone Primary School, Coalville

Hallowe'en

Thee who screams into the night
Darkens my dreams with terror and fright.
Evil has awoken and evil has won
Now I see the greed has begun.

Be it ghoul, be it ghost, be it sprite
All will be revealed by the moon at midnight.
The empty streets will soon be full
Get read, get set, it's time for trick or treat fun.

Thee who screams into the night
Is not a ghoul, not a ghost or a sprite
But is my little brother
Dressed up for a Hallowe'en night!

Demi Nicole Cooper (10)
Thringstone Primary School, Coalville

Nature, Nature, Nature, What Do They Do?

Play around, touch the ground, fly around,
Pop out of your hiding place.
Nature, nature, when will it end?
Nature, nature, they all have a friend.
Nature, nature, I think now it will end.
Nature, nature, I'll show my friend.

Jessica Pharo (8)
Thringstone Primary School, Coalville

The Silly Snake

I found a snake
It was a very silly snake
I caught it on my garden gate
Funnily enough the silly snake could even bake
So I got it to make me a cake
A scrummy chocolate cake
Sad enough . . . the snake was fake!

Courtney Cliff (10)
Thringstone Primary School, Coalville

Friends

F riends are important to our lives.
R edge has a friend.
I sobel has a friend.
E lena has a friend.
N elson has a friend.
D anny has a friend.
S o everyone has a friend.

Fay Henderson (7)
Thringstone Primary School, Coalville

Cat And Kitten

A kitten on a wall watching all
the leaves that fall.
As I watch and stare
the kitten looks but doesn't care;
But he falls off the wall
because he's small
as he climbs up the wall.

Chloe Mensah
Thringstone Primary School, Coalville

My Pet's A Monster

My pet's a monster, he is very nice indeed
But when it comes to table manners he is very much in need.
He will pick his nose
Then lick his toes
While you sip your cup of tea
But please don't forget,
He's a monster just like you can see!

Bethany Russell (10)
Thringstone Primary School, Coalville

Horses On The Beach

H ooves galloping,
O n the sandy shores,
R earing, splashing
S houts of joy,
E veryone who owns a horse,
S hould join me!

Natasha Kinton (8)
Thringstone Primary School, Coalville

Senses

Sight
A flying pig two metres off the ground
With a squirrel on its back. What a scene it set
The unusual thing it was
Sight.

Taste
The smooth crumbs of a muffin on my lips
The melted chocolate on my tongue
My taste buds exploding,
Taste.

Smell
A rotten apple half eaten
With an old smelly boot all damp and wet
I was disgusted, what some people do!
Smell.

Sound
A jet fighter in the sky
Then suddenly a bomber appears in the mist
I was full of fear
When it was coming towards me.
Sound.

Ben Smallwood (9)
Thurlaston CE Primary School, Thurlaston

Joy

Joy feels like love, happiness and fun,
Joy is like all the good times in your life are in one,
Joy is the goodness of all things and the happiness of the
world have become one.

Joy is a tweet of a curving bird in the wonderful blue sky,
Joy, the most wonderful emotion with love and happiness.
Joy is relaxing.

Lloyd King (10)
Thurlaston CE Primary School, Thurlaston

I've Sensed Fear

Fear is something that creeps about at night,
It is one of your biggest nightmares.
It's blacker than coal, darker than night
And as cold as an Atlantic iceberg.

As it touches your lips you shiver and shake,
You tremble at the bitter and sour taste.

The smell of fear is foul and smelly,
Like the sewers beneath our feet.
It makes your nose shrivel up like a raisin
And is enough to make any man drop dead.

Fear is rough, slimy and horrid,
It is the monster from deep down below.

A noise louder than a drum,
As powerful as a clap of thunder,
The noise of fear is terror and scary
And will burst both of your eardrums.

It is a sight you will never forget,
A sight you will always remember
And is as bad as being hung over
A hot, blood-red, bubbling cauldron.

Sarah Kelly (10)
Thurlaston CE Primary School, Thurlaston

Love

Love is yellow shining down on laughing children.
Love is hanging around all the time at Christmas and
the times we are jolly.

It feels soft as a cotton blanket which has fallen on you.

It smells like ice cream, chocolate, candyfloss and sweets.

It tastes like a rosy red apple and banana all yellow.

Cara Boulton (9)
Thurlaston CE Primary School, Thurlaston

147

Is Your Courage Still Strong?

Courage is like a candle, holding itself together until the other one drops melted wax.
It tastes of bitter pain as you stand up to be brave.
You see the vision of a blank look in the enemy's eyes.
The sound of thunder rattles through your eardrums and makes you stronger in the power of your heart.
Your hand floats to the ground like a feather floating down to the jewelled grass,
But then it feels like spikes cut open your hand as you die
down more.
Courage smells of fire as it grows up into you and as it pulls you down to make you more vulnerable to the enemy.
Courage is like black, as your pupils turn to ashes,
for when you die down.

Rebecca Green (10)
Thurlaston CE Primary School, Thurlaston

Joy Of Life

Joy is as happy as the sun on a summer evening.
Joy is green like a calm day by the stream
And joy is white like a polar bear slipping and sliding on the ice.

Joy smells like the cooking of a professional chef or the
scent of roses.
Joy feels as soft as a silky blanket or a pillow with the fur of
a koala bear.
Joy tastes like a crumbly chocolate muffin on the tip of my tongue,
my taste buds exploding
And joy sounds like the softening music of the cello in an orchestra.
It truly stands out from the crowd.
Joy is soothing.

Vincent Woodhouse (10)
Thurlaston CE Primary School, Thurlaston

Silence Surrounding Our World

Silence is white, like a dim winter morning,
It smells like it is emerging through time,
It tastes like a fresh new day and a fresh new year.

Silence feels calm and peaceful, as if all the
children have left the playground.

Silence is the best feeling,
It might be a snowy evening with your family,
A time on your own,
A stroll along the beach with your dog.
Have a time to be alone.
Does it feel the way I've described it?

Amy Thorne (9)
Thurlaston CE Primary School, Thurlaston

Fun

Fun is when a friend comes to play round or go to the park.
Fun is when you have a brilliant party and stay up all night.
Fun makes my tummy rumble when I am happy.
Red is a happy colour and it is very lucky and it is my
favourite colour.
How lucky is that?
Fun is going to the cinema with your friends and watching
a brilliant movie.
Fun is where you get what you want and do what you want
and go wherever you want.
Fun is having a wonderful day doing what you want.

James Davies (10)
Thurlaston CE Primary School, Thurlaston

The Sadness

Sadness feels like you are freezing to death on a cold winter's day
And you don't even have anything to cuddle up to.

It tastes sour and leaves a nasty flavour in your mouth.

Sadness is a dark cave in the middle of the night
You can hear the voices of your past friends whispering
behind your back
And the memory of your family who are no longer here.

Sadness is a horrible feeling to have
It turns you into a lonely cold-hearted person.

Katie Houseman (10)
Thurlaston CE Primary School, Thurlaston

Silence All Around Me

The wonderful warmth of my family
Sitting on the sofa on a winter's evening.

In church, praying to God
As silence surrounds us.

Silence is all around me as I plunge
Into a great book.

In a rowdy classroom I close
My eyes, then silence fills my mind.

Phoebe Edmondson (10)
Thurlaston CE Primary School, Thurlaston

Wonder

Wonder is light blue like the sky on a hot day,
Wonder tastes tropical like exotic fruit on a desert island.
Wonder starts faint and turns into a loud echo.
Wonder can smell like a red rose in a garden on a summer's day.

Carina Barber (9)
Thurlaston CE Primary School, Thurlaston

The Joy In You!

Joy is when you get the perfect present meant for only you.
It's when you see your family beaming happily down on you.
Joy is when you help others then see their smiling faces,
When people get together and care for each other.
Joy is when you meet someone new who likes everything you do.
The joy within your heart is the thing that matters most
of all in you.
It's as if you're in Heaven.

Rebecca Pope (10)
Thurlaston CE Primary School, Thurlaston

Anger Is . . .

Anger is a tiger demolishing its prey in the
dematerialising moonlight.
Anger horrifies even the most valiant of us.
Anger is a raging storm defeating everything in its path.
Anger disgusts the eyes of everyone.
Anger brings down the boldest of us.

Joseph Seale (10)
Thurlaston CE Primary School, Thurlaston

Love

Love is red, like a fire burning,
Love is like kisses in the air,
Love feels soft like a fluffy blanket.
Love tastes of chocolate melting in your mouth - delicious.
Love smells of flowers in a meadow.
Love is with me wherever I go.

Olivia Hine (9)
Thurlaston CE Primary School, Thurlaston

Sadness

Sadness is black as a dark night curling on a car.
Sadness tastes like vegetables when they're cold.
Sadness smells like a pipe shooting out gas.
Sadness looks like the silver moon blowing up.
Sadness feels like a spiky spear.
Sadness sounds like lots of people crying in a cave.

Alex Whyley (10)
Thurlaston CE Primary School, Thurlaston

What Is Courage?

Courage is bright scarlet,
Like a heart about to perform somersaults.

The fragrance of courage
Is enough to make a poppy bloom in the sweet smell of spring.

Courage is a sparkling memory in my mind!

Amy Houseman (10)
Thurlaston CE Primary School, Thurlaston

Silence

Silence is like snow falling down on the treetops
Silence is beautiful, like good memories
Silence is as bright as a star
Silence is happy with joy

Silence is just beautiful.

William Thompson (9)
Thurlaston CE Primary School, Thurlaston

What is Anger?

Anger is black, dark and dull.
It's as fierce as a lion breaking free from his cage.
Anger makes the heart bleed, makes your lungs explode.
Bitter and salty like over-cooked fish.
Shivering, anger attacks your body.

Isabelle Nest-Coleman (10)
Thurlaston CE Primary School, Thurlaston

Peace

White like a dove floating in the midday zephyr,
Fluffy as a teddy bear waiting for a hug,
Sometimes gentle, sometimes faint,
Like a tidal wave it drowns out the darkness.
Peace is strong.

Alanah Lenten (10)
Thurlaston CE Primary School, Thurlaston

Love

Love is sweet like lavender, quiet and peaceful in the garden.
Love tastes like a delicious apple pie warm in my mouth.
Smooth but bitter as it flows down into my stomach.
The smell of lovely tulips makes me feel as calm as a feather
Floating down onto the jewelled grass in my back garden.

Anna Sutton (10)
Thurlaston CE Primary School, Thurlaston

Fun

Fun is gold like the sun streaming down.
Fun is like a roller coaster ride
Fun feels like sand between your toes.
Fun smells like tarmac on the playground floor.
Fun tastes like sweet, smooth chocolate.

Peter Reeves (10)
Thurlaston CE Primary School, Thurlaston

Joy Feels Like

Joy feels like exploding party poppers in a party in the
middle of winter.
Joy tastes like sweet raspberries ripening in the sun.
Joy is red, like poppies glistening in the sun.
Joy looks like clear acrobats jumping and twirling in the air.

Anna Benton (9)
Thurlaston CE Primary School, Thurlaston

Joy

Joy is fun, happiness, love and goodness
Joy is like all the amazing funny things,
Joy is all the good things in life and all the happy things,
Joy is goodness, goodness makes the world come together as one,
Joy is fun, happiness, love and goodness.

Matthew Draycott (9)
Thurlaston CE Primary School, Thurlaston

Silence

Silence is like peace flowing across a cold icy river
Silence is white, like a cloud floating in the blue sky
Silence smells like the cold refreshing air on a winter's morning
Silence feels like a blanket of stars covering the night sky.

Nicole Davies (9)
Thurlaston CE Primary School, Thurlaston

Fun

Fun is when you ride a roller coaster, exciting and scary.
Fun is zooming fast on my quad bike, mud on my face and back.
Fun is riding my bike, skidding on the path.
Fun is having a friend round to play on the Xbox 360.

Charlie Batson (9)
Thurlaston CE Primary School, Thurlaston

Sadness

Like a nightmare that will always haunt you
Like a tidal wave drowning out the light
Like running your hand along a prickly fence full of stabbing nails
Like someone screaming, full of agony and anger.

Taylor Shilcock (9)
Thurlaston CE Primary School, Thurlaston

Rainstorm

Drip-drop, drip-drop.
It's rain, it's raining, what a beautiful sight.
Let's go and play outside.
It is as big as a world shower.

Splish-splash, splish-splash.
The trees are swaying like waving at me.
Plip-plop, plip-plop.
There are some puddles that look like
Millions of circles.

The rain is not stopping!
Bigger and bigger
Faster and faster.
Quick, back inside the rain is too heavy.
Bang! Boom! Goes the thunder.
The rain is hitting the ground
Like shooting machine guns.
The river is raging.

Suddenly! The rain has stopped.
The clouds disappear.
It makes a beautiful rainbow!

Ammar Farooq (10)
Welbeck Primary School, Nottingham

Happiness

Happiness is many colours like a rainbow in the sun.
Happiness tastes like chocolate ice cream which melts in my mouth.
Happiness smells like a big glass with lots of flowers of
lots of colours.
Happiness sounds like birds singing in the morning.
Happiness reminds me of when my brother was born.
Happiness feels like an angel flying around people and bringing
them happiness.

Aleksandra Chudy (10)
Welbeck Primary School, Nottingham

156

Waterfall

A waterfall flowing
All you could hear
Splish, splash, splosh.
The waterfall tumbling
Pouring water.

The river looked like
A big ocean.
Rain falling
Like pins and darts
Coming down fast.

Beautiful sunshine
River meets the ocean
Waves sparkling and bouncing.
Splish, splash, splish, splash.
A beautiful rainbow.

Holly Branford (9)
Welbeck Primary School, Nottingham

The Sea

Huge waves out at sea
Boats struggling, waves too high
Roar, roar, roar.

They can see shore
Row to the land
Pull, pull, pull.

Raining hard
Like a machine gun
Crash, crash, crash.

Sky gets dark
Night is here
Home, home, home.

Daniel Dicks (9)
Welbeck Primary School, Nottingham

River's Journey

Splash! The river goes down.
Down the high rocks it goes.
It sees the deer herd resting
Under the green trees.

Over the trees where the sun
Is glowing like a night lamp
And sugary white clouds
In the light blue sky
The ducks come down
Landing in the water
Going away when the river goes far.

And so it goes having adventures
Splashing and bashing all the way
Till it meets the sea.

Kinga Sitkiewicz (9)
Welbeck Primary School, Nottingham

Happiness

Happiness is the sight of smiles all around the world.
It is the feeling of a rainbow in your heart.
The smell of sweet flowers and the sound of a music box.

Happiness reminds you of the good times and the most shared
moments of your life.
It reminds you of your 10th birthday with your friends and family.
Happiness is the feeling of a newborn life, or a fresh start.

Happiness is like the taste of honey but only in the mouth.
The sound of someone's laughter
Or the sound of someone's tears rolling down their cheeks
like a waterfall
But it's only the tears of joy.

Anita Panahi (12)
Welbeck Primary School, Nottingham

Rain

Crash down on the rocks
Booming and bubbling
When the sun goes down
The water feels silky like a water slide.

Boom crashing on the rocks
Flowing on the ground
Drip-drop
Like an arrow in the night.

Darting, flowing, falling
With the water on the rocks
Splish onto the ground
Like a dart in a dartboard.

Saskia McCormack (8)
Welbeck Primary School, Nottingham

River

A river flows gently across the stream,
Splatting, splashing, smashing.
Rain falls, drops and stops,
Crashing waves sparkling blue.

Suddenly the stream turns into a big waterfall,
The fish swim and hurry before the water crashes everywhere
But turning the water.

The sea calms down, the ocean clears out.
But the pond is black and dark.
The bubbles start to rise but, *splat, splat, splat.*
Everywhere is wet and dry.

Oley Taal (9)
Welbeck Primary School, Nottingham

Frustration

Frustration feels like a raging war inside you that you are constantly losing.
Frustration tastes like a hot curry, burning your mouth to dust.
Frustration smells like the ashes from a smouldering fire that has burned for a thousand years.
Frustration sounds like an angry crowd, all shouting at once.
Frustration looks like a ferocious bull which is in the mood to kill.
Frustration has a colour that can only be described as bloodthirsty red.
Frustration reminds me of a ghost, always seeking revenge.

Hakeem Stewart (10)
Welbeck Primary School, Nottingham

Waterfall

The waves coming sliding down the cliff
Swish, swish, swish
Smashing rocks below
Swish, swish, swish
Booming down on the ground
Swish, swish, swish
The power smashing
Swish, swish, swish
Never stopping always going
Swish, swish, swish, swish.

Alicja Balambilayi (9)
Welbeck Primary School, Nottingham

Sadness

Sadness is blue like a teardrop falling from a child's eye.
It feels like fireworks exploding in your head and you can't
get rid of it.
Sadness tastes like someone feeding you too much junk food, then
you feel sick inside.
It looks like people are hiding away their lives, hiding away
from their predators.
Sadness sounds like a weeping angel from Heaven.
Sadness is all kinds of things but mostly sadness is hurt.

Charlotte Harrison (10)
Welbeck Primary School, Nottingham

Sadness

Sadness is like a roller coaster going up and down and you can
never get off.
Sadness is blue like a teardrop that just fell on a child's pillow.
Sadness feels like someone has just stabbed you in the heart.
Sadness is like a long road of unhappiness that never ends.
Sadness reminds me of the time my grandmother died in my
father's arms.
Sadness tastes like dirty water children in Africa drink.

Riyan Perdawd (10)
Welbeck Primary School, Nottingham

Anger

Anger is a red ball of fire burning inside me,
It is two cars crashing together.
Anger displays the colour of red,
It smells like a burning house.
Anger reminds me of getting hurt,
It tastes sour, I just want to get it out of my mouth.
Anger looks like a river of dead people.

Jake Cumberpatch (11)
Welbeck Primary School, Nottingham

Confusion

Confusion is many colours, illuminating deep inside my body.
It feels like everybody taking over my head.
It sounds like a choir whispering a melody in my ear.
It reminds me of a memory which I didn't understand.
How did I get here?
It tastes like a bundle of flavours burning in my mouth.
It smells of various things which I can smell with a sniff.

Qasim Hussain (10)
Welbeck Primary School, Nottingham

Jess' Head

In it there is a German shepherd puppy
And a project
For doing away with swimming lessons

And there is
Shopping
Which shall be first.

And there is
An entirely new DS
An entirely new chocolate bar
An entirely new pair of shoes.

There is a room
That tidies itself.

There is an art pencil and paper.

There is numismatics.

What I believe is that ideas
Never end just grow and grow in your head.

There is much promise in the circumstance
That so many people have heads.

Jessica Nicholson (10)
Wolvey CE Primary School, Hinckley

Jasmin's Head

In it there is a Sainsbury's shopping bag
And a project for
Doing away with washing-up.

And there are
Great games
Which shall be first

And there is
An entirely new school
An entirely new TV
An entirely new class

There is a pig
That flies

There is a multiplication grid

There is an invertebrate

And it just cannot be trimmed
I believe that only what cannot be trimmed is a head.

There is much promise in the circumstance
That so many people have heads.

Jasmin Ghale (11)
Wolvey CE Primary School, Hinckley

Mitchell's Head

In it there is a football
And a project for
Doing away with school lessons.

And there is family
Which shall be first.

And there is
An entirely new bird,
An entirely new dog,
An entirely new football.

There is a pond
Flowing upwards.

There is a number line.

There is a playground.

And it just cannot be trimmed
I believe that only what cannot be trimmed is a head.

There is much promise in the circumstance
That so many people have heads.

Mitchell Fury (11)
Wolvey CE Primary School, Hinckley

Max's Head

In it there is a bike
And a project for
Doing away with my next-door neighbour.

And there are karts
Which shall be first.

And there is
An entirely new ice cream
An entirely new pizza
Entirely new chips.

There is a super pig
That can fly.

There is a ball
There is a personality

And it just cannot be trimmed
I believe that only what cannot be trimmed is a head.

There is much promise in the circumstance
That so many people have heads.

Max Pritchard (10)
Wolvey CE Primary School, Hinckley

Katie's Head

In it there is a gleaming spotlight
And a project
For doing away with washing-up.

And there is
An entirely new pasta sauce
An entirely new walk-in wardrobe
An entirely new red carpet.

There is a pig
Flying with green wings.

There is a best-selling story.

There is intensification
And it cannot stop
I believe dreams cannot stop.
In a head
There is a sparkling future
Because so many people have heads.

Katie Haughian (10)
Wolvey CE Primary School, Hinckley

Ben's Head

In it there is a street dancing club
And a project
For doing away with literacy lessons.

And there is golf with my dad
That shall be first.

And there is
An entirely new school
An entirely new pizza with cheese
An entirely new TV in the classroom.

A tree that talks.

There is a pencil and crayons

There is a micro computer

And I believe it just cannot be trimmed is a head
There is much promise in the circumstance
That so many people have heads.

Ben Thomas (10)
Wolvey CE Primary School, Hinckley

Kenny's Head

In it there are guns
And a project for
Doing away with school.

And there is money
Which shall be first.

An entirely new chocolate
An entirely new skateboard
An entirely new football

There is chocolate
That doesn't make you fat
There is a computer.

And it just cannot be trimmed
I believe that only what cannot be trimmed is a head.

There is much promise in the circumstance
That so many people have heads.

Kenny Goodwin (10)
Wolvey CE Primary School, Hinckley

Katie's Head

In it is a black and white puppy
And a project
For doing away with picking up dog poo.

And there is a horse which shall be first.

And there is an
Entirely new hairstyle
Entirely new food menu
Entirely new world.

There is a car that can drive to space
There is an art painting that was painted by a dog.
There is antiphonal
And it just cannot be trimmed
I believe that only what cannot be trimmed is a head.

There is much promise in the circumstance
That so many people have heads.

Katie Amies (10)
Wolvey CE Primary School, Hinckley

Young Writers Information

We hope you have enjoyed reading this book - and that you will continue to enjoy it in the coming years.

If you like reading and writing poetry drop us a line, or give us a call, and we'll send you a free information pack.

Alternatively if you would like to order further copies of this book or any of our other titles, then please give us a call or log onto our website at www.youngwriters.co.uk.

Young Writers Information
Remus House
Coltsfoot Drive
Peterborough
PE2 9JX
(01733) 890066